"Smart Ways to do Things"

Nature has figured out incredibly smart ways to do things. Biotechnology harnesses this ingenuity and puts it to work for our benefit. By understanding how biological systems work and applying this know-how to solve problems, we are now able to identify and treat many diseases, develop crops that can thrive in the cold Canadian climate and use computers to help crack the mysteries of the genetic code. We can harness bacteria to produce medicines, extract metals from rock and clean up toxic spills. And the future of biotechnology holds countless new possibilities!

It is my pleasure to introduce this series of career products to young people across Canada. These tools should help take some of the mystery out of biotechnology and open our eyes to the changing role of science in the workplace. There are many fulfilling career opportunities in biotechnology, and Canada continues to experience a shortage of skilled biotech workers in areas such as research and commercial development. The Biotech Career Guide is designed to highlight the wide variety of exciting and challenging jobs - from accounting to zoology - that are available in the many growth industries applying this technology. I hope you enjoy it and it leads you to choose a career in biotech!

Biotechnology
Human
Resource
Council

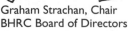

Graham Strachan, Chair
BHRC Board of Directors

Table of contents

■ Getting Products Out There 78

... sales and marketing, manufacturing and field work.

■ Taking Care of Business 104

... administration and regulation.

■ Dr. Michael Smith: A Nobel Ambition 132

This profile of a Canadian Nobel Prize winning scientist is more detailed than the rest. It shows the path that leads to great scientific achievement. Geniuses are made not born!

Training 135

Biotech Training Programmes

List of Biotech Resources

Repertoire of Interviewees 151

Index of 50 profiles 161

5

How to use this guide

● **What is the biotechnology industry?**

For the purposes of this book, the "biotechnology industry" refers to private and public companies, associations, governmental agencies, universities and individuals doing work in the domain of biotechnology.

● **Profiles:**

What are they?

The Profiles give you an inside view of the life and work of 50 individuals working in biotechnology. You'll see what their jobs are, what skills they need and how their work fits into the bigger picture of biotechnology. The Profiles are not necessarily representative of all the individuals who work in the same field or occupy the same position. They are based on the personal experience of each subject and are intended as references only.

● **Date of publication**

A date is included at the end of each profile indicating when it was written. Biotechnology is a relatively new industry and is in constant evolution, so the information in each profile — particularly with respect to scientific aspects — must be interpreted with care.

Example :

(09/98)

● **Career Summaries:**

➼ **Career Tag:**

At the end of each profile a tag indicates what sector of biotech each interviewee works in: health, agriculture, aquaculture, forestry or environment. Career Tags are meant as references only; they do not necessarily apply to the work of a given company or organisation as a whole. In cases where an interviewee's work either does not fall into a particular sector — or covers many — no tag appears.

Example :

HEALTH

➼ **Job Title:**

These titles are based on job description information provided by BIOTECanada Human Resource Council and Personnel Systems, a Human Resource firm in Ottawa, Ontario.

Example :

Bioinformatics Programmer

➼ **Job Category:**

This refers to the category the interviewee's work falls into: research and development, clinical research, sales and marketing, manufacturing and field work, quality control, or administration and regulation. This classification of positions was based on information provided by the Career Planning and Employment Centre of McMaster University.

Example :

Research and Development

➼ **What programmes I did**

This is a list of the academic programmes each interviewee completed, either before or after beginning work in his or her occupation. The list should not be interpreted as a set of definitive requirements for a given occupation.

Example :
■ What programme(s) I did:

Ph.D. in Computational Chemistry, McGill University, Quebec
B.Sc in Chemistry from Concordia University, Quebec

● What are other routes to this position?

These are suggestions of other possible training or professional paths leading to a given occupation. In most cases, this information was provided by our interviewees. It in no way constitutes an exhaustive list of the training requirements for someone interested in a given field.

Example :
■ What are other routes to this position?

Other programmers are either computer scientists, mathematicians, engineers or physicists.

● Skills and qualities you need for the job

This summary of the skills and qualities required for certain jobs will help readers match their own interests and talents with those of workers in particular occupations or fields of work. The list is not exhaustive and should be used as a reference only.

Example :
■ Skills and qualities you need for this job:

- need computer and math skills
- must have background in chemistry and biology

● Salary:

The salary figure following each profile is an AVERAGE SALARY for given positions across Canada. This information was collected by the human resource consulting firm Personnel Systems in collaboration with BHRC. The figure should be interpreted with care: salaries may vary depending on the size and type of company and the region in which an individual works.

Example :
■ Salary

64 123$

● Training:

➤➤ Biotech Training Programmes

A list of college and universities offering biotech-related programmes. This list is drawn from a survey conducted by Dr. William Mak and Dr. John Clement called "Biotechnology Training in Canada." The survey was conducted to determine how science programmes offered in Canada are meeting the needs of the biotech industry. The institutions included in the survey and the programmes listed DO NOT constitute an exhaustive list of programmes for training in biotechnology. This list does not include Master's and Doctoral programmes and it should be interpreted as a reference tool only. To get further information on available training, please consult "List of Biotech Resources".

➤➤ List of Biotech Resources:

This is a list of associations where you can find up-to-date information on biotechnology, and includes both national and regional biotech bodies. Also included: a list of career information resources to help you get started planning your own career!

➤➤ Repertoire of Interviewees

This is the name of the interviewee, his or her job title at work and the address, phone and web site of the company he or she works for. Interviewee's job titles often differ from the job titles at the beginning of each profile. Such disparities happen for a variety of reasons, but mainly because job titles differ from one company to the next. We have tried to find interviewees whose work corresponds as much as possible to the job titles and job descriptions provided by BHRC.

Biotech in Focus

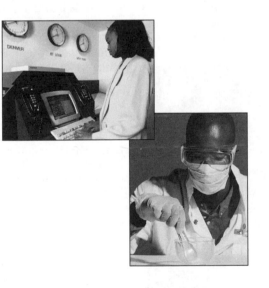

What is Biotechnology?

▶By Tracey Arial

The term "biotechnology" was first used in Canada in 1983. Fifteen years later, Canadian researchers and companies are using biotechnology to tackle challenges in human health, agriculture, acquaculture, forestry and environment.

Saskatchewan and Alberta's wheat industries owe their success to a turn-of-the-century plant breeder named Sir Charles Edward Saunders. In 1909, Saunders introduced a special variety of wheat which matured a week faster than normal. The reason? The sooner wheat matured, the less likely it was to be destroyed by the early frost common in Western Canada. His variety, called "Marquis" wheat, produced higher yields and made better bread. By 1920, more than 90% of our Prairie farmers were growing it.

Photo : Courtesy of Agriculture and Agri-Food Canada

Sir Charles Edward Saunders

Saunders knew that the inherited characteristics of plants, like colour, texture, and stiffness, travelled from one generation to

another. He figured out that he could "create" stronger or faster-maturing plants by choosing only the best plants to pollinate and using their seeds to grow new plants. Saunders worked by trial and error. He chewed on individual kernels to test for elasticity and he baked tiny loaves of bread to test for volume, finally choosing the kernels that would bear the "Marquis" name.

> **Although human beings have been using biotechnology for millennia to produce things like bread, beer and yogourt, the actual term biotechnology was only coined in the late 70's.**

By using science to solve a problem, Saunders became one of Canada's earliest biotechnologists, although he was never called that when he lived. The term "biotechnology" is a combination of the Greek term "bio," which means "living organism", and "technology," which refers to an applied science that solves problems or improves the human condition. While scientists seek knowledge to satisfy their curiosity, biotechnologists start with a concrete goal and use science to achieve it, adapting living organisms like humans and other mammals, insects, plants, fungus and yeast bacteria.

> **While scientists seek knowledge to satisfy their curiosity, biotechnologists start with a concrete goal and use science to achieve it.**

What Charles Saunders didn't know was that while he was creating better wheat, he was actually choosing plants with the best genes. Genes, the foundation of all biotechnology, are groups of special molecules called nucleotides which are made of phosphate, sugar and either a purine (adenine or guanine) or a pyrimidine (cytosine or thymine). The nucleotides are chained together to form long strands of deoxyribonucleic acid (DNA). Two matching strands of DNA are intertwined in a double helix pattern. The number and order of nucleotides in each gene determines heredity characteristics, such as the colour of mushrooms, how fast yeast reacts and whether a person has blue or brown eyes. These genetic instructions pass from parent to offspring.

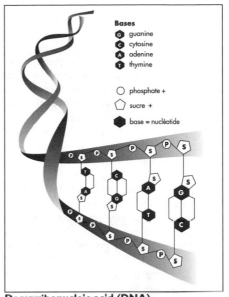

Bases
G guanine
C cytosine
A adenine
T thymine

○ phosphate +
⬠ sucre +
⬡ base = nucléotide

Deoxyribonucleic acid (DNA)

Although human beings have been using biotechnology for millennia to produce things like bread, beer and yogourt, the actual term biotechnology was only coined in the late 70's.

Fifty years after Saunder's experiments, scientists identified genes and began to study their chemical makeup. 1973 was the dawn of the modern biotechnology era. That year, American scientists Stanley Cohen and Herbert Boyer successfully transferred genes from an African clawed toad to bacteria. That proved that genes could be transferred between completely different organisms. Their discovery opened up possibilities for all sorts of experimentation.

Although human beings have been using biotechnology for millennia to produce things like bread, beer and yogourt, the actual term biotechnology was only coined in the late 70's. By then, scientists had learned to manipulate hereditary traits manually by transferring genes from one organism to another.

Health was the first sector in Canada to be touched by biotech, and is still the largest.

The term "biotechnology" was first used in Canada in 1983. Now, nearly a hundred years after Charles Saunders' success, biotechnology is being used in roughly five economic sectors: health, agriculture, aquaculture, forestry and environment. In each sector, companies and researchers are looking for ways to solve specific problems.

Health was the first sector in Canada to be touched by biotech, and is still the largest. Canadian discoveries include Humulin, a human insulin for diabetes patients. Insulin used to be extracted from animals, but Eli Lilly used Cohen and Boyer's gene-transferring technique to make a certain bacteria, E. coli, produce this human insulin. Another Canadian company, Nexia Biotechnologies Inc., recently "created" a genetically modified goat, Willow, that will produce human drugs in her milk. Another company, Algène Biotechnologies, is looking for the gene that causes Alzheimer's disease. If they find it, they might be able to cure the disease by modifying the gene.

Another company, ID Biomedical Corporation, is using genes to detect bacteria and viruses deadly to humans, such as tuberculosis. Researchers are modifying foods to give them medical properties, and research is underway to alter pigs' genetic make-up so that they can grow replacement organs and blood for humans.

Forestry biotechnology finds techniques to increase lumber production and quality. Silvagen Inc., for example, has developed ways to make trees grow faster, resist pests and diseases and produce better-quality wood. Another company, Forbes Medi-Tech Inc., converts forest by-products into valuable drugs that treat high cholesterol levels and keep arteries from clogging.

Environmental biotechnology involves finding better ways to clean up disasters and decontaminate land, water and air. Biogenie Inc., for example, uses live biological agents to decontaminate chemical-laden soil. Other companies are adding enzymes to cattle feed to reduce air pollution caused by methane, a gas released by grazing cattle.

Biotech efforts in aquaculture centre on fish and aquatic plants. So far, researchers have created genetically-modified salmon that grow faster and bigger than other salmon. They are also producing vaccines and other methods to cure fish, particularly farmed fish, which get diseases more often than fish in the wild.

Biotechnologists in agriculture are looking for new ways to produce more food at a lower cost. The first genetically-altered food product to receive government approval in Canada was Chymosin, in 1990. This new enzyme replaces calf rennet, calf's stomach lining used in cheese making. Chymosin costs half as much and is more readily available. Elsewhere, a Saskatchewan company has developed a vaccine that protects livestock from shipping fever, a common cause of death.

It's too bad Charles Saunders isn't alive today. Instead of baking tiny loaves of bread and chewing on kernels, he'd probably be carefully studying the genetic structure of wheat in a computer.

A team of researchers from Canada's National Research Council, Novartis, Monsanto Canada Inc. and several universities are now following in Saunders' footsteps to create genetically-improved wheat. But instead of carefully pollinating wheat plants in the fields, they are identifying the genes they want to replace on computers in the lab. They then use a little "gene gun" to shoot appropriate genes through the cell walls of the wheat plant. And instead of only being able to add genes from other varieties of wheat, they can add genes from any other plant or animal.

It's too bad Charles Saunders isn't alive today. Instead of baking tiny loaves of bread and chewing on kernels, he'd probably be carefully studying the genetic structure of wheat in a computer. There's no doubt that in this modern world of high-tech biotech tools, his discerning nature and powerful skills of observation would lead to important new discoveries. Luckily, there are lots of other Canadians following his example! ∎

What's Going on in Canada?

► by Liz Warwick

Meet Willow, the Canadian biotechnology wonder kid. Willow may look and act like an ordinary baby goat, but she's Canada's first transgenic goat. She carries a gene from another species inside her cells — in her case, a human gene. This gene means Willow can produce a human protein in her milk to be used to make treatments for our diseases.

Created by the Montreal company Nexia Biotechnologies Inc., Willow is one of the many innovations putting Canada on the map as a world leader in biotechnology. From pneumonia vaccines to cancer treatments to genetically-altered salmon that grow faster and bigger, Canada's biotech industry has come a long way since 1983. That was the year the Canadian government created a National Biotechnology Strategy to help the industry grow and develop. Today, only 15 years later, Canada has just under 300 companies employing about 11 000 people primarily engaged in biotech. Almost half of these firms work in healthcare; about a quarter work in agricultural biotech, another 12 per cent focus on the environment, and the rest work in other fields including forestry and aquaculture. These employment levels are just the tip of the iceberg. The industry expects to employ more than 18 000 people in the year 2001. As well, the impact of the biotechnology industry and its products translate into many additional forms of employment including legal, financial, consultant work, food processing and manufacturing and, of course, university research.

Photo : Sean O'Neil · Nexia Biotechnologies

Willow, Canada's transgenic livestock animal

Biotech business is growing, as is Canada's reputation worldwide. Canada has the second-largest concentration of biotech companies in the world, after the United States. A Canadian company, BioChem Pharma Inc., situated in the Montreal area, discovered and commercialized 3TC, a drug radically improving the lives of people infected with HIV. This recent discovery has catapulted Canada onto the world biotech stage.

And why is Canada becoming a biotech leader? "Over the years, we have developed a strong and highly reputable science base," says Joyce Groote, President of BIOTECanada and a long time observer of Canada's biotech industry. "For example, Canadian scientists have discovered about 25% of the genes responsible for human diseases and disorders known today." The United Nations rates the University of Saskatchewan as one of the world's top agricultural centres. Toronto has 13 major teaching hospitals, including the world-renowned Hospital for Sick Children where researchers are working on gene therapy for a variety of diseases.

13

Canada's system for regulating biotechnology products — the set of rules we have developed to protect humans, animals and the environment — is also among the best in the world, says McLaughlin.

The industry does face challenges, however. One of these is a shortage of qualified workers. Canadian schools are training the right kind of skilled workers, but probably not enough. A 1995 study by Human Resources and Development Canada predicted that the biotechnology industry would create 6 000 to 10 000 new jobs by the year 2000. This demand for workers means there will be many opportunities for young people interested in biotech careers.

To better understand what kinds of jobs will be available and where, here's a cross-country overview.

ATLANTIC CANADA

The majority of Atlantic Canada's biotech activity is in the aquaculture field. From transgenic salmon which grow four to ten times larger than regular salmon, to tests that identify fatal toxins in shellfish, the ocean remains a primary focus for many of the companies in New Brunswick, Nova Scotia, Newfoundland and P.E.I. Important developments are also taking place in health, forestry and agriculture.

William Mills, executive director of BioNova, the Nova Scotia Biotechnology and Life Science Industry Association, calls the region "a biotechnology cluster about to happen". Just 10 years ago, there were only a handful of companies working directly or indirectly in biotechnology in Nova Scotia. Today, BioNova has more than 70 members.

Unlike traditional chemotherapy, in which cancer-fighting drugs expose the patient's whole body to dangerous chemicals, photodynamic drug therapies use a laser to activate the drug only at specific sites.

Nova Scotia success stories include Efamol Research Inc. focusing on essential fatty acids which the human body requires, but does not produce naturally. Efamol Research produces an oil from the evening primrose plant, which helps the body make fatty acids. The company sells the oil as a "nutraceutical" — a natural product believed to be beneficial to human health. The company has also used its fatty acid research to develop eczema and osteoporosis treatments .

Efamol Research is also working on photodynamic drug therapies for cancer treatment. Unlike traditional chemotherapy, in which cancer-fighting drugs expose the patient's whole body to dangerous chemicals, these treatments use a laser to activate the drug only at specific sites.

In New Brunswick, significant research is underway in areas of forestry and agriculture. "New Brunswick is a leader in a process called conifer somatic embryogenesis, a process that allows researchers to identify faster and larger growing trees," says Roger Bernier, Executive Director of BioAtlantech. New Brunswick is also a leader in the study and production of potatoes. Researchers in the province are working on ways to make transporting, planting and growing seed potatoes easier and faster.

QUEBEC

Quebec is a major player in the biotechnology field. The province has 31 per cent of Canadian biotech companies, and ranks tenth world-wide in biotech revenues. The total work force in the "core" biotech companies has doubled in the last four years, to nearly 1 700.

Quebec, particularly Greater Montreal, is best known for its biotech breakthroughs in health care. According to a study by Quebec's Ministry of Industry and Commerce, 55 per cent of the province's biotech companies focused on health. The presence of important companies like BioChem Pharma Inc., Merck Frosst

Canada Inc., Bristol Myers-Squibb company and others have helped make Quebec a biotech stronghold.

While Montreal houses about 70 per cent of the province's biotech companies, the Quebec City area — including Laval University's research facilities — is also home to a number of up-and-coming biotech firms. In suburban Ste-Foy, AEterna Laboratories has made news with Neovastat, a promising new cancer treatment that may block the growth of cancerous tumours. Neovastat is made from molecules found in shark cartilage.

> **"People are paying more attention to their health and they're interested in natural treatments."**
>
> **— Serge Hébert, director of the Technopole Agroalimentaire of Saint-Hyacinthe.**

Health dominates in Quebec biotechnology, but it is not the only promising sector. Serge Hébert, director of the Technopole Agroalimentaire of Saint-Hyacinthe, says nutraceuticals (medicines derived from food products) are the coming trend. "People are paying more attention to their health and they're interested in natural treatments," he says. "Nutraceuticals cost much less to develop than traditional medicines."

Quebec companies are also working on ways to produce higher-quality food and other products for animals. Researchers are looking for ways to add particular bacteria to animal feed which helps animals digest their feed better, reducing farmers' costs.

In all sectors, Quebec companies are very optimistic about the future. "There's so much potential in the industry," says Diane Boisvert, director of the Quebec Bio-Industries Association. Skilled workers, she adds, will be in demand for many years to come.

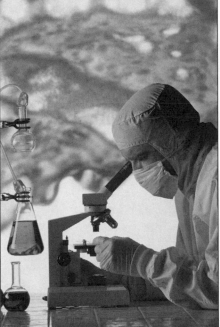

Photo : Photodisk

ONTARIO

Ontario's biotechnology sector has two very strong areas: health and agriculture. Matt Buist, a biotechnology business development manager for the city of Toronto, explains that most health-related biotechnology is done in Toronto. He estimates that about 60 per cent of Toronto biotech companies focus on "therapeutics" or treatments for various diseases. Another 30 per cent are working on diagnostics and another 10 per cent focus on bioengineering.

Health care is a leading sector in Ontario in large part because of Toronto's world-class medical facilities, says Matt Buist. Toronto ranks as the fourth largest medical complex in North America, and has produced many important biotech breakthroughs. Researchers at Toronto's Hospital for Sick Children discovered the gene that causes early-onset Alzheimer's disease — the first step in developing a treatment. Toronto is also home to the

Molecular Biology and Human Genome Research Centre, located at Mt. Sinai Hospital. The Centre, which focuses on creating new treatments for diseases through genetic research, is one of only five of its kind in the world.

Outside Toronto, the province's main biotechnology centre is Guelph, home of Ontario Agri-Food Technologies, where research focuses on agriculture. Harsh Canadian winters mean the area of cold-resistant crops is receiving much attention.

To develop hardier grapes, researchers have inserted a gene from a Canadian wild grape into the wine grapes.

The Niagara peninsula winery Château des Charmes is working with the University of Guelph to develop cold-resistant grapes. Dr. John Paroschy, the winery's research scientist, explains that when temperatures drop to -25 C, over 50 per cent of a vineyard's grapes can be damaged. To develop hardier grapes, researchers have inserted a gene from a Canadian wild grape (which grows in Manitoba and can survive very cold temperatures) into the wine grapes. Grape testing has just begun

but Paroschy is hopeful. "If we are successful, it would reduce the damage farmers face each year. Sometimes there's so much damage to the grapes that the farmers lose just about all the crop."

The Ottawa region is another fast-growing biotechnology centre. Ken Lawless, executive director of the Ottawa Life Sciences Council, an agency which promotes the region's biotech and life science sector, says "There is a tremendous amount happening here, from neuroscience to nuclear medicine to cancer treatments and cardiovascular devices and treatments." Lawless estimates that 18 000 people are directly and indirectly employed in the biotech and life science sector. Apoptogen Inc. is a promising Ottawa company working on new treatments for stroke, cancer, Parkinson's disease and glaucoma. The company is trying to understand why apoptosis — normal genetically programmed cell "suicide" — doesn't occur in the case of certain diseases, like cancer. They hope this discovery could lead to a treatment.

PRAIRIE PROVINCES

Biotechnology and agriculture have been a winning combination in the Prairie provinces, a region now recognised as a world ag-biotech leader. The products and discoveries coming out of these Western provinces will have an impact on food production around the world, says Peter McCann, president of Ag-West Biotech Inc. The world's population is growing at a rapid pace, he notes. However, the Earth has a limited amount of areas suitable for food production. "Ag-biotech can help us get more production from the existing land without polluting," McCann says. Testing is going on for faster-growing, hardier crops with a higher nutritional content. Canola is a particularly good example. Saskatchewan has one of the world's largest projects to study canola, a plant that yields a high-quality cooking oil for humans as well as animal feed (from the crushed seeds). Researchers are working on canola varieties that can grow in drier, less fertile areas, grow more quickly and are resistant to certain fungi that normally destroy the plant.

> **"The ag-biotech industry is growing like crazy and it's going to need skilled people to keep it going."**
>
> **— Peter McCann, president of Ag-West Biotech Inc.**

Calgary-based SemBioSys Genetics Inc. is using a genetically-altered canola plant to produce hirudin, an anti-bloodclotting agent that can reduce heart attacks.

Researchers at Saskatchewan's Plant Biotechnology Institute are working with researchers at the Unviersity of Saskatchewan to alter the molecule in wheat that determines starch stickiness. Countries like China and Japan represent a huge potential market for this genetically-altered wheat, which is used for making certain Asian noodles. The researchers are also working on ways to extract the extra starch and use it to create biodegradable products like cups and plates.

For McCann, there's never been a better time for ag-biotech than now. "The industry is growing like crazy and it's going to need skilled people to keep it going."

BRITISH COLUMBIA

Vancouver is British Columbia's biotechnology hub. About 90 per cent of the province's biotech companies are located in the greater Vancouver area. For most of these companies, health care, particularly therapeutics, is the main focus. But the fact that B.C has growing aquaculture, agriculture, forestry and environmental sectors makes it unique in Canada.

While British Columbia houses about 20 per cent of Canada's biotech companies, its health sector is particularly strong for several reasons, says Theresa McCurry of the British Columbia Biotechnology Alliance. "We have an extremely strong infrastructure," she says. "We have three universities in the area, several teaching hospitals and a strong clinical trials network." (Clinical trials allow companies to test their products in a controlled and regulated way).

Forestry is a still a small but growing biotech sector. Theresa McCurry suspects that the sector will get a boost in the coming years from forestry companies, because they are more and more interested in biotech products.

One of B.C.'s leaders is QLT PhotoTherapeutics Inc. QLT produces Photofrin, the only drug of its kind in the world, to treat various cancers. When Photofrin is injected into a cancer patient, the drug slowly accumulates in the malignant tumour cells. Then a laser is passed through the tumour activating the drug to destroy the tumour. QLT is also developing phototherapy treatments for other diseases including age-related blindness, heart disease and autoimmune diseases.

British Columbia has produced one very important player in the forestry sector: Silvagen Inc. The company has developed a special process to create large quantities of high-quality tree seeds. The seeds produce faster-growing, disease-resistant trees which yield better quality wood. These qualities are important for reforestation — replanting areas where trees have been harvested.

LOOKING AHEAD

There is no doubt the Canadian biotechnology industry is a growing field. However, future growth depends on people making early decisions to pursue a career in biotech. Those currently working in biotechnology say it's critical that young people learn about the opportunities available in the field. One way to do this is through an innovative national programme sponsored by Pasteur Mérieux Connaught Canada — the Connaught Student Biotechnology Exhibition, an annual science competition held in St. John's, Halifax, Montreal, Ottawa, Toronto, London, Saskatoon and Vancouver.

"No matter which aspect of biotech interests you, it's important to learn about the range of jobs available."

— Matt Buist, board member of the Toronto Biotechnology Initiative.

Students who want to participate in the Biotechnology Exhibition submit a proposal for a biotech project to their local organising committee, usually made up of representatives from biotech industry associations, government agencies, educational institutions and biotech companies. If the proposal is accepted, the student receives a grant for the project as well as an established researcher's assistance. The completed projects are shown at the Biotechnology Exhibition. The top five or six projects receive prizes which include $1 000 scholarships.

No matter which aspect of biotech interests you, it's important to learn about the range of jobs available, says Matt Buist, vice president of the Toronto Biotechnology Initiative. "There's a lack of understanding about the variety of jobs in the biotech area," he says. Whereas people often associate biotechnology with researchers in lab coats, the industry has openings for many kinds of workers. Regulatory affairs — the process of getting new drugs and treatments to market — will become increasingly important, Buist says, since many companies have only recently reached the point where they have a product to sell.

Biotech workers of the future will need a strong grounding in science and business alike, claims William Mills of BioNova. "We need to get business into the science departments and science into the business departments," he says. If researchers want funding, they will need to be able to talk about the commercial potential of their research — its potential benefits and applications.

For people willing to commit their time, energy and skills, biotechnology promises significant rewards.

But biotech companies are also facing a critical shortage of managers who understand science and can steer a company from its start-up days (with heavy investments in research and development) through the process of marketing and selling a new product.

It will be a challenge, industry spokespersons say. But for people willing to commit their time, energy and skills, biotechnology promises significant rewards. Whether creating a vaccine to protect children from disease or developing plants able to weather winter storms, biotech workers can look forward to a future of discovery, creativity and satisfaction. ■

The Biotech Career Guide

is
brought
to you
by:

Conseil de ressources humaines en biotechnologie
Biotechnology Human Resource Council

Youth Employment Strategy — Stratégie emploi jeunesse

Canada

with the collaboration of the following biotech associations:

AWB

Bio East — Newfoundland's Biotech Initiative

ONTARIO Agri-Food Technologies — From Discovery to Profit

BIO ATLANTECH

AQB — ASSOCIATION QUÉBÉCOISE DES BIO-INDUSTRIES — QUEBEC BIO-INDUSTRIES ASSOCIATION

BIOTECanada

tBi

TBN The Biotechnology Network

FBCN

Enterprise PEI

Bio Nova Nova Scotia's BioIndustry Association

BCBA BC Biotechnology Alliance

OTTAWA Life Sciences COUNCIL

**Minister of
Human Resources
Development**

CANADA

**Ministre du
Développement des
ressources humaines**

As the Minister of Human Resources Development Canada, I want to congratulate the Biotechnology Human Resource Council (BHRC) on this new series of career awareness products.

Biotechnology is a dynamic, global industry. It is creating a growing demand for more people with specialized skills in scientific research, technical support, marketing and management. I support and welcome this initiative to encourage young Canadians to learn about these career opportunities and to know how to enter the field.

The information contained in the products developed by the BHRC can be used by students, teachers, counsellors and industry mentors. The occupations being presented are the ones which employers themselves believe will offer the greatest potential for those young people making career decisions.

I am proud that my department is working in partnership with the BHRC in offering young Canadians the opportunity to pursue long-lasting careers that will help make Canada a world leader in the 21st century.

Pierre P. Pettigrew

Finding your Place in Biotech

▶ By Laurie Barlow Cash, Career Counselor

Wondering what it takes to get a job in biotech? Worried that you need to be a scientific genius to get into the industry? You should put your fears to rest, because biotech work really has one basic requirement: an interest in science.

As you'll see in the 50 profiles, people with very diverse backgrounds opt for careers in biotech, and for many different reasons. Biotech workers must like science, yet not all are scientists - some are doctors, lawyers, veterinarians, writers, technicians, librarians, computer programmers, business school graduates and more. Some are driven by the desire to push forward the frontiers of scientific discovery. Others want to tackle specific problems, like environmental disasters or diseases. Some are driven by a social mission like curing disease, spreading information or educating people about science. And still others find biotech a challenging and rewarding outlet for their skills, whether these involve collecting information, working on computers, marketing products, organising people, working with animals or writing contracts.

Biotech workers perform or use research into nature to create solutions to problems. Their work cuts across five industrial sectors: agriculture, aquaculture, environment, forestry and health.

For anyone contemplating a future in biotech, some post-secondary education will be necessary. But not all jobs require a PhD in science! If you are interested in biotech but not sure where to start, you must start out with the basics: understanding yourself and your own talents and interests. And the key to this, as all the experts stress, is information.

One thing you need is a good understanding of what biotech is. Biotech workers perform or use research into nature to create solutions to problems. Their work cuts across five industrial sectors: agriculture, aquaculture, environment, forestry and health. It is important to know what's going on in each sector, but also to understand that the lines between sectors are becoming fuzzier: animal research is used for human medications, and agricultural issues are often environmental issues. People working in biotech these days must thrive on change!

The next thing to understand is what people in the biotech industry actually do. Biotech work falls into six "areas": research and development, clinical research, quality control, manufacturing and field work, sales, marketing and administration, and regulation. Work in each area is quite different, and each requires certain skills and personality characteristics.

What do Biotech Workers Do?

RESEARCH AND DEVELOPMENT (R&D)

Biotech Research and Development workers spend their days creating, testing and applying new biotechnologies. Technicians and technologists, trained at college, often do R&D work in the laboratory, but most workers in R&D have university science degrees, and many have Ph.D.s, — the highest possible level of academic training.

R&D scientists must be analytical thinkers and enjoy solving technical problems. They must also be self-starters — since they are rarely supervised — and versatile.

The heads of R&D departments all have Ph.Ds. Completing a Ph.D can take seven or eight years — good training in more than one way, because patience is a must for R&D. "In R&D you can't be looking for short-term results," comments Natalie Nossal, Manager of McMaster University's Science Cooperative Education department. "The person who enjoys R&D is curious, patient and imaginative and doesn't get frustrated easily."

R&D scientists must be analytical thinkers and enjoy solving technical problems. They must also be self-starters— since they are rarely supervised — and versatile. "We have our hands in many different areas," says Peter Miles, Research and Development Manager at McNeil Consumer Products in Guelph, which develops new Tylenol products. Peter and his staff have to make sure that Tylenol products won't spoil in their packaging (by analysing packaging materials and processes) and are safe and effective.

There are currently more jobs in Research & Development than in any of the other five biotech areas. Many biotech workers get their start there and move on to other areas, says Dr. Eleanor Fish, an Associate Professor of Medical Genetics and Microbiology at the

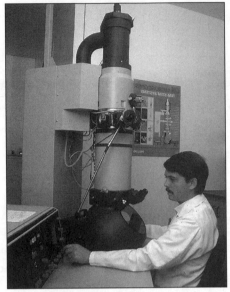

Photo : Saint-Luc Hospital

University of Toronto. "You can stay in the science, start your own company or work for one, become a team leader, then a director, or you can move out of the science, for example into Regulatory Affairs."

CLINICAL RESEARCH

Finding out "if what was cooked up in the lab is actually going to help people" is the thrill of working in clinical research, says McMaster's Natalie Nossal. Clinical research workers travel to research sites, often spread out across the country, to organise clinical tests of new drugs on humans. Like their R&D colleagues, most clinical research people have degrees in science or health science (often nursing), but the work is quite different.

If you enjoy working with people and travelling, clinical research is exciting work.

Clinical research work is a study in contradictions: it's research work, but not in a lab, and not even in one place. "You interact with people a lot. You need to have energy to deal with people," according to Natalie Nossal. Clinical researchers are comunicators, persuaders, report writers and presenters, and their work "is a teamwork, large-scale, long-term kind of thing". If you enjoy working with people and travelling, says Natalie Nossal, it's exciting work.

SALES AND MARKETING

Even people who haven't studied chemistry and biology can get into biotechnology. "Do what I did," says Jeff Passmore, Executive Vice President at Iogen Corporation, a 60-employee company developing alternative energy sources. Jeff is in charge of Sales and Marketing, finding partners to help develop and distribute Iogen products. He spends his days (and many nights) meeting with people from government, the general public and other companies working with Iogen to "get them all on side."

Biotech sales and marketing people are movers shakers and the ultimate persuaders — the kind of people who do what other people say is impossible. "They have to be excellent comunicators and like taking risks," says Jeff Passmore. Sales and marketing people work more with people and ideas than complex technical problems or equipment. "Expressive, amiable and outgoing people tend to go into marketing and sales," says Dr. Murray McLaughlin, President of Ontario Agrifood Technologies.

A science degree is preferable but not essential for Sales and Marketing work. Iogen's Jeff Passmore studied Political Science, English literature, Economics and Journalism, which he says helped his creative thinking. But Dr. Eleanor Fish says sales reps, particularly in the pharmaceutical industry, need to know their science. The physicians who buy pharmaceuticals have many drugs to choose from now, she notes. "Unless a salesperson has some science background to answer doctors' questions, how will he or she sell a drug?"

QUALITY CONTROL/ASSURANCE

Many people compare Quality Assurance/Quality Control workers to the inspectors in mystery novels. They are responsible for setting standards for how something is made and making sure those standards are achieved. Part watchdog, part detective, they must make sure biotech products, very often pharmaceuticals, are made correctly, and are safe and reliable at all times.

Because biotech products directly affect human health, QA/QC work is very important. The people who do it take their responsibilities very seriously. They must be conscientious workers who value human health and safety, and who faithfully observe, report and act on what they see — even if this means more work and challenges for their company. Both creative and curious, they are sticklers for detail. The rewards? Seeing things done right, and knowing their products are trustworthy.

Photo : Corel Library

ADMINISTRATION AND REGULATION

Biotech is science, but it is also business. As such, it needs all the players that businesses need: people to count the cash and pay the bills (accounting staff), to find and hire the right people (human resources people), to talk to the public and the media (public relations or communications staff), to move supplies in and products out (purchasing, materials handling and logistics staff), to handle any legal problems (legal affairs people, often lawyers), to supply information (librarians and information professionals) and to look after computers and computer systems (information systems workers). All these roles are usually referred to as "administrative jobs".

Two types of administrative jobs that are especially important in biotech are Intellectual Property and Regulatory Affairs.

Intellectual Property workers safeguard their companies' ideas and products. They get patents to legally protect their companies' products. They also advise researchers on how to develop products that won't infringe on someone else's patent, or "intellectual property".

Regulatory Affairs workers play a major part in getting new products (often drugs) approved. They pick up where clinical research workers leave off, putting all the information from clinical trials into documents submitted for government approval to make and sell a product. Regulatory Affairs workers are often former scientists who made a change after ten or more years of doing research. "They love working with information and details, and love the challenge," says U of T's Dr. Eleanor Fish.

MANUFACTURING AND FIELD WORK

Workers in manufacturing and field work roles love getting their hands dirty and seeing things happen. They work with manufacturing equipment and on-site material, observe, troubleshoot and solve any problems. They often have specialised training including engineering (taught at university) and engineering technology (taught at college). Both these academic disciplines use science to solve concrete problems.

"Field Work" describes biotech work done outdoors, like that of Chris Juneson, an Environmental Engineer with Biotechnik in Toronto. Biotechnik uses microorganisms to clean up or "remediate" contaminated soil or water. The first thing Chris does is perform tests at Biotechnik's labs to figure out which microorganisms to use. Then he supervises setting up special equipment on the site, including wells, piping, fans and microorganisms.

Like others who do field work, Chris describes himself as a "practical type of person". His advice to people interested in work like his? "If you enjoy a wide range of responsibilities, love being outdoors a lot and doing hands-on stuff, you'll like this work."

SO HOW DO I GET STARTED?

For high school students interested in pursuing any of these six areas, what's the first step? "The McDonald's University isn't a bad place to start", says Natalie Nossal, referring to the low-skill jobs where most teenagers get their first work experience. "You get an appreciation for what is expected of you, of how to work with a team and how to respect your team members and your business clients. These things aren't trivial."

You don't need to read scientific journals to get a lot of information on what's going on in the field. Anybody who reads the paper will know how big an issue biotech is right now.

According to Peter Miles of McNeil Consumer Products, volunteering and getting involved in community organisations looks good on a biotech résumé. "These experiences show that a person knows how to have fun. If you can't have fun, you're going to approach everything in life as a chore." Well-rounded people with sports and hobbies are more interesting to any company, he says. "People who have many interests tend to do better than those who

are totally focused. They can take their mind off something for a while and leave it idle, and that's when the breakthrough ideas come."

Beyond being well-rounded, keeping up on current issues and biotech's latest break-throughs is crucial. It's not enough to look at biological science as just something in a textbook, says Natalie Nossal. "Read the paper to see how it's real." Getting into the information habit will also show employers that you have the right kind of curiosity — not just about science, but about how biology and chemistry affect our daily lives. "You don't need to read scientific journals to get a lot of information on what's going on in the field. Anybody who reads the paper will know how big an issue biotech is right now. If science students aren't keyed into this, I wonder about their chances."

Because biotech products begin with reseach, it's important for students to know which research areas are hot. Biotechnology is a quickly-changing field. "Ten years ago if you were doing anything in cancer research you could find a job anywhere. Now the trend is towards finding ways to manage inflammatory diseases such as arthritis," says U of T's Dr. Eleanor Fish. The Internet is a great tool for high school students inter-ested in biotech trends and opportunities, she says. Company Web sites will describe their current research projects, while bigger companies' Web sites often advertise sum-mer employment opportunities for students, sometimes called "fellowships" or "sponsor-ships".

As for high school, college or university courses essential for getting into biotech, the jury is still out. The most relevant courses at the moment are university-level courses in cell biology, immunology and genetic engineering. These subjects are par-ticularly important, says Dr. Eleanor Fish, because they are crucial to getting jobs in the health sector — by far the biggest sec-tor in Canada. "Biotechnology in human health is really about understanding the immune system and cloning some of those components," she says. The most successful people in biotech have tended to go in with graduate degrees, often Master's degrees or Ph.D.s. "A graduate degree will make you very marketable," she says.

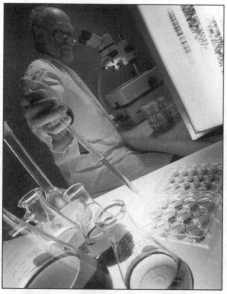

Ontario Agrifood Technologies' Dr. Murray McLaughlin, once Deputy Minister of Agriculture for Saskatchewan and considered a leader in bringing biotech to Canadian agriculture, agrees. "The more education you have, the more control you will have over your own future." But pursuing years of university training in science blindly isn't necessarily a wise move either, he warns. "Students have to have a gut feel for what they want to do." He himself completed a Ph.D. and thinks it probably helped him on his career path — but only because he was passionate about it. "If you want the Ph.D. you should do it because you want to, not because you think it's going to earn you more money."

> **"You have to be very open to moving around, but the beauty of this career is that it's very portable. You can take your credentials anywhere."**
>
> **— Dr. Eleanor Fish**

As for biotech job opportunities, the experts see many contrasts. There is now intense competition for some jobs but shortages of qualified people for others. In pharmaceutical research, for example, U of T's Dr. Fish notes that the job market is very competitive, and getting a job depends on a candidate's mobility. "You have to be very open to moving around, but the beauty of this career is that it's very portable. You can take your credentials anywhere."

At the same time, some companies are actually having difficulty finding qualified workers. Molecular biologists, for example, are currently in high demand in all biotech areas. Murray McLaughlin compares the present shortage to the computer field. "Employers have to be willing to pay a significant salary or they just aren't going to get them," he says.

Still, all the experts do agree on one very important point: biotechnology is a new industry that will definitely grow and create jobs in the future. Again, Ontario Agrifood's Dr. McLaughlin likens the situation to the computer industry, which had "pioneers" long before it started to create a lot of jobs. The same goes for the biotech industry. "Many of the jobs at the moment are for highly-trained scientists because they are the ones that develop the technology," says Dr. McLaughlin.

If McLaughlin and others like him are successful in developing Canada's biotech industry, there will soon be more demand for workers in the related areas, says Jeff Passmore. "We will need scientists to keep pushing the science ahead, engineers to build the projects, and economists to work on the policy front."

Environmental biotechnology is a sector which holds a lot of promise. While demand for workers in the renewable energy field has been weak over the past few years, Jeff Passmore of Iogen is certain environmental biotech has a bright future. The sheer scale of environmental challenges facing Canada should translate into more environmental biotech jobs in the future, he says. In his opinion, government, the public and now even insurance companies are becoming keenly aware of the need to reduce greenhouse gas emissions, and biotech will play a large role in responding to global warming and climate change.

How do you turn anxiety about change into a valuable tool? One way to do this is to focus on learning, says McMaster's Natalie Nossal.

The crucial lesson for students who want to work in biotech is to get very comfortable with change. "Biotech companies come and go," says Dr. Fish. "Unless people are prepared to accept that change, this field is not for them." Even on a day-to-day basis, biotech workers must deal with a great deal of change and disruption. As Jeff Passmore puts it, "Chaos tends to be a management tool these days" in the industry.

But just how do you turn anxiety about change into a valuable tool? One way to do this is to focus on learning, says McMaster's Natalie Nossal. "Students need to learn how to learn, so that when they are out there in the constantly changing workplace they'll know how to move forward and constantly grow in their science," she says. Another approach is to develop creativity, which equips people for making change, rather than just reacting to it. Not surprisingly, biotech experts say changing careers within the industry is also a major trend.

Getting into biotech may sound like a challenging prospect, and it is. You have to be well-rounded, well-informed, ready for constant change, creative and prepared to work in a competitive environment.

Biotech doesn't fit neatly into our traditional thinking. It also doesn't fit neatly into universities' traditional science departments anymore. Many departments are merging and getting new names, in part because of government funding cuts to universities, but also because of biotechnology's impact. As U of T's Dr. Eleanor Fish puts it, "The life science departments are all coming together, and what's driving it is that the work people are doing is really crossing the scientific disciplines. It's no good to have a specialisation in only one area of science. You must have a broader awareness." The most successful people in

Photo : Marc Lajoie - MAPAQ

27

Photo : Courtesy of BioChem Pharma

biotech research, says Dr. Fish, are the "very creative ones who can look at what's already out there, plus the new findings, and pull it all together into something new."

Getting into biotech may sound like a challenging prospect, and it is. You have to be well-rounded, well-informed, ready for constant change, creative and prepared to work in a competitive environment. You have be flexible, adaptable and willing to work in an area of science that has no clear boundaries. It may sound like a lot of work and no fun, but according to Natalie Nossal, that's far from the case.

Working in biotech, she says, means working in an industry full of enthusiastic and passionate individuals. "Energetic, excited and confident" are the words she uses to describe Canadian scientists — who are anxious to help young people get involved, she adds. "Canadian scientists have stopped waiting for the government grant money to roll in and are looking for more creative ways to work. It's a really exciting thing for young scientists to see happening, and a real change. You can see the excitement in our students because the excitement the entrepreneurs have is contagious. You can see the scientists acting as mentors, and you can see the lights go on." ∎

Biotechnology Gateway

http://strategis.ic.gc.ca/bio

The Gateway is a comprehensive resource which brings
biotechnology information from across the globe
right to your screen!

...Find out what biotech companies are doing and
who to contact for the job you want

...Learn about innovations and technological
applications of biotechnology

Biotechnology Science Centre

http://strategis.ic.gc.ca/learnbiotech

 Do You Know...

✦✦✦ About the most famous sheep in history?
✦✦✦ How to fight crime using DNA?
✦✦✦ About microbes that feed on toxic waste?

Check out the website that combines nifty graphics with
straightforward explanations of some of the hot new
biotechnologies of the 21st Century!

Life Sciences   Direction générale
Branch   des sciences de la vie

Canadä

Profiles

Photo : PPM, Montreal

"The Computer Chemist"

Chris Williams' passion for computers began when he was 16 and his father brought home one of the early PC's for him to program. "I played with it for about a year and a half," he said. "Then I never did anything in computers again...until I started my Ph.D." Today, Chris is one of only 3 000 people in the world with a doctorate in Computational Chemistry. His job as customer support scientist at Chemical Computing perfectly combines his love for science with his love for computers.

What I do

Chris is a chemist, but he doesn't mix up solutions in beakers and test-tubes; he mixes them in the computer instead. Actually, the computer does the mixing. Chris tells the computer how to mix by adding instructions to scientific vector language, a computer software created by Chemical Computing.

Scientific vector language stores data on what millions of chemicals look like and what they do. Scientists use it to match up carbohydrates, proteins and other molecules like a puzzle. It saves them time and

money because it allows them to see which molecules fit together before trying to mix the actual substances together in a test tube. It also allows them to see why some chemicals mix well while others don't.

Merck Frosst, Bristol-Myers Squibb and other major pharmaceutical companies use the software to sift through information collected by robots synthesising up to 10 000 drugs daily. Other clients use it to identify proteins or improve the properties of paper and plastic.

As a customer support scientist, Chris adds new information to the software for clients when needed. He also answers any questions or problems clients have by interpreting results and checking computer code, the instructions that tell the software what to do.

Chris also attends conferences, gives presentations and contacts scientists individually. He must keep up with new scientific literature in biology, physics, mathematics, chemistry and medicine and keep track of who is who in the scientific world.

What skills
do I need?

"I'm a scientist, so I try to understand as much about the universe as possible." This intense curiosity has defined Chris' career from the beginning. He never cared about following the traditional path to a science career.

Normally, a chemist follows a Bachelor's degree with four years of study towards a Ph.D. Chris put off a scholarship to work for an explosives company for two years instead. He wanted the experience.

When he went back to do his Ph.D., he chose a field that would force him to learn physics, computers and math as well as traditional chemistry, because he liked the challenge. While studying he met an organic chemist who wanted to work with him. That led Chris to study biology, medicine and oncology (the study of tumours). In the last couple of years, he began teaching elementary pupils how to use computers and taught chemistry part-time for a CEGEP.

It took five years for Chris to get his Ph.D., but he now has a job that satisfies his curiosity. "What I like about my job is that I end up being a bit of an expert in a variety of fields," he says. "I'm not a complete expert in any field, I'm more of a 'jack of all trades'."

What is
the work like?

Chris' hours are flexible. He usually arrives at the office between 8:30 and 10:30 and spends most days at his computer, which is in a cubicle beside four other programmers.

The first part of his day is dedicated to communicating with clients. "I start my day checking emails from customers. If they have any problems with our software product, or if they have any questions, I write back to them by email and tell them what certain results might mean or describe certain aspects of the software. I call them occasionally just to see how things are going, to see if they have any problems or questions and make sure that they're happy with the product. That's the support part of the job."

Once that's all out of the way, Chris sits at the computer to write code. First he thinks about what a scientist normally does in the lab and then he puts it into logical steps that can be programmed into a computer. To do that, he might have to go to the library or he might visit the experts in their labs. Usually he emails or talks to them on the phone.

"What makes my days interesting is that first I might talk to someone who designs paper, then to a designer for Merck Frosst, then to a designer who designs proteins for another company, then to an oncologist who designs cancer drugs... I don't get bored. I can't—because I never know enough."

▶By Tracey Arial (09/98)

HEALTH

Bioinformatics Programmer
Research and Development

■ What programme(s) I did:

Ph.D. in Computational Chemistry, McGill University, Quebec
B.Sc in Chemistry from Concordia University, Quebec

■ Average salary

$55 000

■ What are other routes to this position?

Other programmers are either computer scientists, mathematicians, engineers or physicists.

■ Skills and qualities you need for this job:

- need computer and math skills
- must have background in chemistry and biology
- must be able to explain difficult concepts
- must be friendly

"The Genetic Detective"

Photo : Daniels & Glionna Photography, Toronto

As a bioinformatics scientist, **Yvonne Frater** is like a detective. To solve her mysteries though, she doesn't study people and their motivations; she studies DNA and protein and their behaviour. Instead of "who did it" she tries to find out "what does it do?" And instead of examining evidence with a magnifying glass, Yvonne uses a computer.

What I do

Yvonne works as a bioinformatics scientist at Base4 Bioinformatics, a consulting company doing genetic research for biotech companies. The scientists and computer programmers at Base4 use computers to store, retrieve and analyse biological information such as DNA (the "recipe" molecule that determines heredity) and proteins (the "building block" molecules of living things).

Yvonne's clients are mid and large-size pharmaceutical or biotech companies searching for the genes responsible for hereditary diseases like cancer, Alzheimer's, Parkinson's, asthma, arthritis and certain cardiovascular diseases. Some of Yvonne's clients are taking part in the Human Genome Project whose aim is to sequence all the genes in the human body. Researchers have already identified slightly more than 70% of the 100,000 genes humans are thought to have and stored this information in a database called GenBank.

The ultimate goal of the Human Genome Project is to develop medications or treatments acting directly on specific genes to

either cure or prevent diseases. But first, companies have to figure out which genes play a part in what diseases. Then, when they think they have their finger on the right gene, they patent it so no one else can use the discovery.

That's where Yvonne comes in: using her computer, she compares a client's strand of DNA or a protein sequence with those listed in databases around the world to determine whether it is actually new and unusual and whether it might work in the same way a well-known strand or sequence works. If it is new, she compares it further to find out if the gene might work in the same way a well-known strand does.

Yvonne is a project leader at Base4, meaning she is responsible for communicating all results of the project she is working on to her clients. To do this, she meets with her colleagues to keep tabs on their progress, and then sets up presentations to inform clients of progress. About twice a year, Yvonne also attends conferences where she advertises and markets Base4's products, collects information and networks with others in the industry.

What skills
do I need?

While she was at high school, Yvonne hated math and physics courses. But she knew she wanted to work in science, so she took them anyway. She went on to complete not only a Bachelor's degree, but a Master's and a Doctorate in science, specialising in toxicology and pharmacology.

When Yvonne finished her Doctorate in Biochemical Toxicology at the University of London (England), several U.S. pharmaceutical companies tried to recruit her. But Yvonne had "fallen in love" with Canada during a holiday in Vancouver, and decided to accept a postdoctoral fellowship in Kingston, Ontario. Then she was drawn to the new bioinformatics industry.

"I see life as one big classroom. My challenges are to learn as much as I can on the job, including taking any new courses."

She hasn't been disappointed working at Base4. "Most of the work we're dealing with is at the cutting edge," she says. "It's on the frontier. It's not in textbooks. It's being written as we speak."

To succeed as a bioinformatics scientist, Yvonne says one needs a creative attitude so as to learn from any situation. She attributes her own success to this outlook. "I see

life as one big classroom. My challenges are to learn as much as I can on the job, including taking any new courses."

A bioinformatics scientist at Base4 must also work in secrecy since she is dealing with patent issues. The companies she works for do not want to pass on any information to competitors. She has never been allowed to make her work public. Even her doctoral thesis is classified information! Yvonne collaborated with a major pharmaceutical company to complete the thesis, so anyone who wants to read the results needs the company's approval.

What is
the work like?

Yvonne works in an open-office setting with fellow application specialists and other computer programmers. "We work as a group, bouncing ideas off each other," she says. The team might discuss what they know about databases, or work out the best strategy for discovering more information about a particular strand of DNA or protein.

Most of Yvonne's day is spent at her desk conducting searches or setting the computer to automatically conduct searches and notify her when they're completed. "I spend 99% of my time on the computer. That's bioinformatics!"

▶By Tracey Arial   (09/98)

HEALTH

Bioinformatics Scientist
Research and Development

■ What programme(s) I did:

B.Sc in Pharmacology, University of Liverpool, U.K.
M.Sc. in Toxicology and Histopathology, University of London, U.K.
Ph.D. in Biochemical Toxicology, University of London, U.K.
Post-doctoral fellowship in Biochemistry, Queen's University, Ontario

■ Average salary
$80 000

■ What are other routes to this position?
Any strong biology or biochemistry background.

■ Skills and qualities you need for this position:
- need strong science background
- must have computer skills
- must be organised and methodical
- should be flexible, creative and show initiative

35

Photo : Bryan's Photography, Edmonton

"Thinking Machines"

Scott Fortin is a computer scientist who likes a challenge. Scott is vice-president of software development at BioTools Inc., a company that designs software which helps scientists discover more about how proteins and genes look and act. The challenge? BioTools' software must make routine jobs faster and easier, and enable scientists to study massive amounts of data, or they won't use it. A lot of the responsibility for this falls on Scott's shoulders, because he's the one who hires, organises, and supervises the nine computer scientists who work on the software.

What I do

BioTools computer scientists create a set of instructions which tell a computer how to do a job that a genetic researcher would normally do him or herself. For example, PepTool, BioTool's first piece of software, enables scientists to use computers to find out the sequence or order of amino acids, a key part of genes. So far scientists have loved it. The software has sold so well that Scott's programmers are rushing to finish a DNA sequence analysis software called GeneTool.

Some of the computer scientists at BioTools are programmers. Others are system administrators who help employees solve their problems. Scott is responsible for hiring them all and helping them get their work done. This task takes up about a third of his work time. "I wander around making sure that nobody is stuck on anything and that they're all working well," he says.

Scott spends another third of his time on his own computer, putting his Master's degree in Computer Science to good use by working on the design of software products like PepTool and GeneTool himself.

"I can see that I play an important role. I affect the goals, the strategy and the day-to-day running of our company."

The last third of Scott's job is spent finding business for BioTools by meeting potential clients. These could be scientists who use BioTools software or CEOs and managers from other companies who want Scott's team to design software for them. BioTools is trying to develop a presence as a contract programming company. "I have to meet with other companies to explain the skills we have and eventually bid on their contract."

"It's gratifying for me to work here," says Scott. "I can see that I play an important role. I affect the goals, the strategy and the day-to-day running of our company."

What skills
do I need?

Scott did complete a Master's in Computer Science, but he says he did it for personal interest, not because he thought it was necessary for his job. The programming skills taught in a bachelor's programme are sufficient for computer programming, he says.

What his job requires are good people skills and self-confidence. Scott learned this from personal experience. BioTools was founded by four professors from the University of Alberta. When Scott was first hired, he had just a Bachelor's degree. At first he was intimidated. "I saw mistakes that I predicted happen, but I hadn't said anything about them. The next time, I was more confident and likely to speak up. I eventually realised that there were several questions that I could answer best, even better than my professors. I don't know if I had confidence when I started the job, but I grew into it."

The other quality his job requires is learning ability. BioTools expects their computer scientists to write software properly. It concentrates on teaching them any relevant biology they may need. Scott himself had no background in pure science before coming to work for BioTools and now must be more familiar with certain aspects of micro-biology than microbiologists themselves! "We have access to biochemistry and molecular biology professors who can give us one-on-one, highly focused tutorials on what we need to do."

What is
the work like?

BioTools requires staff to be at the office between 9 AM and 4 PM. Scott works from 9 until 6 or 6:30. Most of his time is spent at his desk or wandering around the other programmers' desks. However some days are taken up with meetings throughout the city. "That part of my job is more free-form, but also enjoyable," he says. Scott also attends conferences in order to keep up with developments on both the computing and molecular biology sides of his job.

BioTools has 30 employees at Scott's downtown Edmonton location. The firm's rapid growth means everyone shares an office. But in order to keep employees from becoming too obsessed with their computer screens, the company has squeezed a dart board and ping-pong table into the premises.

▶By Tracey Arial   (09/98)

HEALTH

Bioinformatics Software Engineer

Research and Development

■ What programme(s) I did:

B.Sc. in Computer Science, U. of Alberta, Alberta
M.Sc. in Computer Science, U. of Alberta, Alberta

■ Average salary

$65 000

■ What are other routes to this position?

A molecular biologist with computer science skills would be qualified to be a bioinformatics software engineer.

■ Skills and qualities you need for this job:

- must have computer science expertise
- must have familiarity with molecular biology
- need a logical, mathematical mind
- must have a desire to learn

37

"A Passion for Plants"

A passion for plants, developed as a young girl working for relatives in a nursery, led **Julie Brais** to choose a biotechnology career. Today, she works as a research technician for Performance Plants, a company working on projects such as improving crops' cold and frost resistance and genetically altering them to increase their yield.

What I do

As a research technician, Julie is involved in isolating certain desired genes in plants. She then introduces them into other plants and then verifies that they are present in the new grown plant's genetic make-up. For example, to make a rose more frost-resistant, Julie would try to find the gene in a plant like crocuses, which makes them resistant to cold, and then insert it into the rose's genetic make-up.

DNA, or deoxyribonucleic acid, is the carrier of genetic information in the nucleus of cells. It contains all instructions required to define an organism and provides instructions for the millions of cellular processes which occur daily. RNA, or ribonucleic acid, plays a role in transferring information from DNA to the cell's protein-forming system. DNA is like the computer program and RNA is the wiring that carries the signals to the different parts of the computer.

To verify if a gene has been successfully introduced into a new plant, Julie collects tissue samples of a grown plant to examine its RNA and DNA. She then performs what's called a "blotting", a process which creates visual evidence of the presence of different genes in DNA or RNA.

Blots are created by putting the isolated DNA or RNA into a dish containing a relatively thick gel. The DNA or RNA is loaded into the pre-cut slots in this gel, the dish is left for 10 to 15 hours for the samples to run into the gel. Then a membrane that looks like a plain piece of white paper is placed on top and left in place overnight, and the DNA or RNA is transferred onto the membrane. In the morning, Julie bakes the gel and introduces P-32, a radioactive agent. "It runs around and sticks to the DNA," she says. P-32 makes the DNA or RNA sample visible on an x-ray film so that Julie can analyse results of the experiment.

What skills
do I need?

To succeed as a lab technician, a strong science background is essential. Julie says having extra experience in experimentation greatly widened her career choices. "I've worked at my family's nursery since I was thirteen, so I have over twenty years experience in agriculture/horticulture."

Julie says that her organisation skills and initiative are some of the qualities that Performance Plants appreciates the most.

Julie says first-hand knowledge of plants is what has kept her fascinated by experimenting all these years. "It's quite amazing to see the change from the plants we had years ago to what we have now. A lot of it is due to scientific studies and I find the manipulation aspect fascinating," she says. "The way the world is going, they say we're not going to have enough food for the population in a number of years. If we don't research how we can manipulate and make our plants produce more, we're going to be in trouble."

A desire to learn, good organisational skills and team spirit are important attributes for a lab technician, according to Julie. "You need to be able to work in teams, be very organised and very co-operative. You also need good laboratory practices, meaning good techniques in your lab work because you work with a lot of chemicals. You have to be careful because you could be endangering yourself or the people around you." Julie says that her organisation skills and initiative are some of the qualities that Performance Plants appreciates the most.

What is
the work like?

Performance Plants is located in the Biosciences Complex on Queen's University campus in Kingston, Ontario. The complex houses a number of biotech companies as well as labs for professors. Julie works in a small lab with four work stations. She says her work environment is a typical lab setting: long counters covered with glassware and equipment to perform her experiments.

A typical day for Julie starts around 8:30 and ends around 4:30. "Some days, I'm here earlier or later. It depends on my schedule and what has to be done. If I'm doing many DNA isolations, then I might be here longer."

She usually organises her schedule a week ahead of time, which is just fine by her. "My supervisor puts me on a team where certain things have to be done and it's up to me to come up with my own schedule."

▶By Christine Daviault   (09/98)

AGRICULTURE

Lab Assistant
Research and Development

■ What programme(s) I did:

Home Economics Diploma, Kentville College in Kentville, Ontario
Horticulture Technician Diploma, Niagara College in St. Catherines, Ontario
Biotechnology Technician Diploma, St. Lawrence College in Kingston, Ontario

■ Average salary

$25 275

■ What are other routes to this position?

Horticulture background, as well as a university degree in Biology or Molecular Genetics. A specialisation in either plant or animal genetics can also lead to this position.

■ Skills and qualities you need for this job:

- need scientific curiosity
- should be comfortable working in a team
- must be able to organise your work
- should have a desire to learn

Photo : Donald Rocheleau Photo, Ville-Marie

"Mr. Yeast"

David Cameron makes his living from yeast. He doesn't bake bread or brew beer. He helps a company called Tembec Inc. use yeast to create alcohol from wood. It's not magic, just good science. And that makes David happy. "I've always been interested in biology on a practical level," he says. "I wanted to produce things."

What I do

David works at a mill which produces wood pulp. The pulp is used to make paper products such as tissues and paper towels. At the mill, thousands of wood chips are dissolved by heating them with chemicals like sulphur dioxide and ammonia. The pulp is removed, leaving a waste water filled with various materials including sugars. Then the water is fermented with yeast to produce ethanol, commonly known as alcohol.

David's job is to make sure the yeast produces the greatest possible amount of alcohol. To do that, he runs experiments in his laboratory to see if different kinds of yeast will produce more fermentation and thus more alcohol. David is also doing an experiment to see if the waste water, once fermented, can produce fertiliser for farm and garden use.

Just steps away from David's laboratory is a small-scale, fully functional pulp mill called the pentose pilot plant, run entirely by computers. In this miniature alcohol plant, David can actually ferment a sample of waste water with a yeast strain and, in a hands-on way, see how much alcohol is produced.

> **"In terms of job opportunities in any of the biological sciences, a Ph.D. is better than just a Master's degree,"** David says.

As the mill's only microbiologist, David is often asked questions about biological materials that build up in the mill's equipment. He'll take samples, study them in the lab, do some library research and try to find a solution to both the immediate problem (getting rid of the stuff) and long-term problem (avoiding the build-up).

What skills do I need?

"In terms of job opportunities in any of the biological sciences, a Ph.D. is better than just a Master's degree," David says, because there are more jobs available at a higher salary for a person with a Ph.D.

But success on the job depends on other skills, he adds. Determination is very important. "At school, you're told 'here's your lab, here's your problem, now solve it.' It's not like that at all in the real world," he says. Companies expect employees to identify and solve problems.

To find out what is happening in the mill, David talks to everyone he meets from supervisors and mill operators to lab technicians. Each of these people knows something valuable about the mill and how it works, David says. By listening to them, he understands more about how to keep the mill running efficiently.

In his laboratory, David usually gets help from two or three assistants. He tries to help them be responsible for their work. "I try to point people in the right direction," he says by getting them to define a problem (i.e. what is this material that we found in a boiler), devise experiments and give people deadlines for completing the work.

What is
the work like?

Variety is the word David uses to describe his work. For family reasons, David tries to keep to an 8:00 a.m. to 5:00 p.m. schedule. The first two hours of his day are always the same. He arrives and meets with his lab assistants to discuss how experiments are going, any problems and what work remains to be done.

At 9:00 a.m., David attends an "operations meeting" where all aspects of the mill's operations are discussed. Then, David meets with his boss to give the latter an update on the lab, the pilot plant and the mill itself.

After that, it's anything goes, David says. "There's just such a wide range of things that I do." He'll work on an experiment in the lab or use his computer to examine results from experiments at the pilot plant. Often, someone from the mill will ask him to check out a piece of equipment that isn't working properly because of some kind of biological material building up. David also spends part of his day writing reports or working on grant applications to come up with funds for more experiments in his lab.

David's enthusiasm for his job shows up in the 50 to 60 hours he works each week. He usually takes work home with him in the evening, and comes in on weekends. For him, it's all part of his belief that employees should give 100 percent. "I've always favoured teamwork and being able to give something back to the company that gives me a job and a paycheque," he says.

▶By Liz Warwick   (09/98)

FORESTRY

Lab Manager
Research and Development

■ What programme(s) I did:

B.Sc. in Biology, Queen's University, Ontario
B.Sc. in Microbiology, University of Guelph, Ontario
M.Sc. in Microbiology and Immunology, McGill University, Quebec
Ph.D. Chemical Engineering and Microbiology, McGill University, Quebec
Industrial Postdoctoral Fellowship (NSERC) with Lallemande Inc, Centre for Food Research and Development, St. Hyacinthe, Quebec

■ Average salary

$64 143

■ What are other possible routes to this position?

Any graduate-level work (at least a Master's) in applied sciences (biology, microbiology, biochemistry, chemistry, environmental sciences, pulp and paper sciences or engineering).

■ Skills and qualities you need for this job:

- must have good research skills
- need background in applied science
- must be able to listen to people
- must be able to set and meet deadlines

41

Photo : Kevin R. Bogetti-Smith, Vancouver

"The Laboratory Life Guard"

If anything enters or leaves the labs at StressGen Biotechnologies, **Rebecca Kennedy** knows about it. As coordinator of facilities, purchasing and safety, Rebecca orders equipment and supplies for the labs and sees that used materials like needles and hazardous chemicals get thrown out safely.

What I do

Rebecca spends more than half her work time on "purchasing", the process of ordering supplies and equipment for StressGen Biotechnologies, a company creating new treatments for infectious diseases and cancer. About 40 people work in the company's labs.

When lab workers need supplies, they fill out a form and bring it to Rebecca. Common items to be ordered include latex gloves, disposable dishes for growing cells and various chemicals ranging from sugar and salt to very hazardous materials.

Rebecca checks to make sure the information on the form is correct. Often there are mistakes. "They might have the wrong item

number or even the wrong catalogue number," she says. "It takes a lot of time to get all the information right." Once she has an order ready to go, she calls the vendors or people who sell laboratory equipment and places the order.

When orders arrive, Rebecca checks to make sure the right supplies were delivered. She then sees the supplies get to the right lab. When hazardous chemicals arrive at the lab, a data sheet is included with information on safety (how to handle the chemical safely, how to dispose of it and the risks involved in using the chemical). Rebecca makes copies of the fact sheets and puts them in binders that are easily available to the lab workers. If a chemical is particularly hazardous, she personally gives the fact sheet to anyone using the chemical.

> "The variety of people I deal with is amazing. You really have to be a people person to do this job."

It's also part of Rebecca's job to give "safety tours" to new employees. She shows them how to handle equipment and materials in a safe way and what to do in case of a chemical spill. She has also written a manual about on-the-job safety for employees.

What skills
do I need?

"You have to be very, very patient and diplomatic to do this job," Rebecca says. She talks with people all day long, either asking them for more information on an order, placing an order or explaining a safety procedure. "The variety of people I deal with is amazing. You really have to be a people person to do this job." The job also demands persistence, she adds. If an order doesn't arrive, for example, Rebecca must track down what happened to it.

Rebecca came to her job with a diploma from the Southern Alberta Institute of Technology. She holds a diploma in Chemical Technology, which she earned in two and a half years after finishing high school. "The programme was really practical," she says. Students learned how to use and maintain a wide variety of machines and equipment used in labs.

Rebecca was hired at StressGen as a laboratory technician responsible for maintaining and purchasing laboratory equipment. To gain experience in other areas of the company, she worked in the accounting office for a while before accepting her current position.

Now that her job includes safety issues, Rebecca has started taking workshops on job safety or "occupational health." She's also working on another diploma in Occupational Health and Safety from the British Columbia Institute of Technology.

What is
the work like?

Rebecca is usually on the job at 7:30 a.m. and finishes around 3:00 p.m. She arrives early because many of the vendors she orders from have offices in the East and are three hours ahead of Victoria, B.C. time.

"This is not a desk job."

She shares an office with two other people: the company librarian and the computer system specialist. All three get lots of people coming in to ask questions, so the office is rarely very quiet. Rebecca says she almost never has a long period of time to herself to work or make phone calls. "People are always interrupting me," she says, adding that she's learned how to stop a project and then pick it up again when she has the time.

However, Rebecca says, "This is not a desk job." While she handles a lot of paperwork, she also talks with all kinds of people and helps solve different kinds of problems every day. "There's so much variety in purchasing and safety."

►By Liz Warwick (09/98)

HEALTH

Lab Support
Research and Development

■ What programme(s) I did:

Diploma in Chemical Technology, Southern Alberta Institute of Technology, Alberta

■ Average salary

$27 036

■ What are other routes to this position?

N/A

■ Skills and qualities you need for this job:

- must have background in laboratory work
- must pay attention to details
- must be persistent
- must enjoy keeping track of information

Photo : Courtesy of BioChem Pharma

"Fine-Tuning Drugs"

Yili Bai fights cancer for a living by helping provide cancer patients affordable medication. Yili is senior scientist at Phytogen Life Sciences, a company that researches, develops and produces generic drugs mainly for breast cancer and lung cancer patients.

What I do

Yili is senior scientist and head of the process development unit, one of the most important departments at Phytogen. She is responsible for finding a way to produce low-cost medications like paclitaxel, a cancer-killing drug derived from tree bark.

Phytogen didn't actually invent paclitaxel. Instead, it bought the patent for the drug from another company. While patents show the ingredients going into a given drug, they don't provide any instructions on how to make it. Yili receives information on how to produce very small samples of medication on a regular basis. Her job is to take that formula, conduct experiments and help find a way to mass-produce those drugs within a given budget and time frame.

Yili starts by performing what is called "chromatography". In short, she breaks down a drug to figure out its active ingredients. After that, she has to scale up, or figure out how to make a new drug from it with the desired effects. It is largely a trial-and-error process, trying different approaches until she finds one that works. "It's like baking a cake," she says. "Making one cake is easy, making ten thousand at a time is another matter."

Finally, Yili is responsible for improving medication by making the active ingredients as chemically pure as possible. She works to remove all inactive ingredients that don't contribute to helping a patient fight cancer.

Yili attends meetings, then prepares a detailed report on how the production department should manufacture the medication, once the lab work and experiments are completed. She sometimes recommends additional studies to develop production equipment, or suggests improvements in current studies.

What skills
do I need?

Curiosity is essential for this career, as are knowledge of biology, chemistry and biochemistry. A B.Sc. degree is the minimum background for work as a junior scientist in the process development unit.

Yili holds a B.Sc. degree in Chemistry from Beijing Medical University. Her perfect marks led her to skip over the Master's right into Ph.D.-level research at the University of Calgary. From there, she did post-doctoral studies as a visiting fellow at Agriculture Canada, under the N-Serc program, and at the University of Georgia.

"The more education you have, the better," Yili says. "It teaches you how to solve problems. It's also better in the long run. There are opportunities for more interesting work and a better salary."

Yili was born and raised in China, and educated in three countries. This experience has given her a unique outlook. "My cultural background has given me a special interest in the healing properties of plants. What I learned at school has given me the ability to use these plants to help improve medication. I also tend to look at a person as a whole when he is sick. Doctors here tend to look at just the symptoms or the area affected."

Yili's job requires effective time-management skills, and the ability to meet deadlines. "Sometimes deadlines are hard to meet because new problems come up unexpectedly The production department needs the information to manufacture the drug and the marketing department needs to sell it."

What is
the work like?

Besides conducting experiments, Yili supervises a team of scientists and ensures the work is done on schedule. It's an intense 40-hour week that begins at 8:30 a.m. and ends at 4:30 p.m., Monday to Friday. "We have a schedule to follow because each day is a little different. We look at the results from the previous day and continue where we left off." Her regular schedule, however, allows her a balanced lifestyle so she can spend time with her husband and young son.

However, most of Yili's work is done in a laboratory, a quiet environment where casual wear and lab coats are the norm. More than one hundred experiments are conducted to determine how one drug can be mass-produced. That information is then given to management and the production unit who determine the equipment needed to produce the medication and its packaging.

"We don't just work to copy a drug, we want to improve its performance," says Yili. "The most rewarding part of my job is finding out that what worked in the lab also worked in production."

▶By Wallie Seto and Sylvain Comeau (09/98)

HEALTH

Process Development Scientist
Research and Development

■ What programme(s) I did:

B.Sc. in Chemistry, Beijing Medical University, China
Ph.D. in organic chemistry, U. of Calgary, Alberta
Post-Graduate Studies at the U. of Georgia, U.S.A.
Post-Doctoral fellowship at Agriculture Canada through the N-SERC programme

■ Average salary

$47 600

■ What are other routes to this position?

Any graduate level work in a pure or applied science such as biochemistry and chemistry.

■ Skills and qualities you need for the job:

- need background in chemistry and biology
- must be methodical and pay attention to detail
- must be able to work independently

Photo : Kevin R. Bogetti-Smith, Vancouver

"Insects by Don"

Back in 1970s, greenhouse growers in British Columbia began to realise that some of the chemical pesticides they were using were dangerous. They called Agriculture Canada, who started looking for alternatives. Agriculture Canada handed the problem over to **Don Elliott**, an entomologist (insect scientist). Don is an expert in developing beneficials, insects that act as natural pesticides themselves by killing insects that eat commercially-grown plants and vegetables. They are possibly the most environmentally friendly pesticides on the planet!

What I do

Don's interest in insects goes back long before he founded his company, Applied Bio-Nomics, to develop environmentally-friendly bug-eating bugs. His fascination began as a child living in the tropics with his parents. He started working for Agriculture Canada at age 15.

Now, as president of Bio-Nomics, Don actually oversees every aspect of operations of his company: research and development, marketing, sales, distribution and customer service. But among the different hats he wears, research and development manager is one of the most important. This job involves keeping track of all the latest news about insects so Don can steer his researchers in the right direction. He spends a lot of time reading, surfing the Web, and going to conferences and conventions for growers and entomologists.

The main task of Don's researchers is to see whether particular insects are effective as predators. The Applied Bio-Nomics research team experiments with the insects in special greenhouses they keep filled with fast-growing tobacco and bean plants. Don has to make sure operations run smoothly. "We practically live in the greenhouses for fear of emergencies like power failures and sudden temperature changes," says Don. "We have to make sure those bugs stay alive."

Don also has to make sure his researchers have enough money to do their work. It can take as long as five years, and can cost at least $100 000, to find out if a particular bug is the right kind of beneficial, and then breed and distribute it. It's Don's job to come up with adequate funding to carry the research projects out. This money often comes from either the federal or provincial government. The growers have a big say in governments' decisions about where to spend research funds, so Don spends a lot of time giving talks to explain his product to them.

What skills
do I need?

Don is an entomologist, and most of the people he works with are either entomologists, or at least have a B.Sc. A research and development manager must know the environment he or she is working in, whether it is a greenhouse or a laboratory. A manager must also have very specialised knowledge of his or her field, whether it be plant or animal biology. In Don's case, managing research also means knowing the particular problems of growers in order to offer them viable solutions.

A research and development manager must be able to put together research teams to work on different projects. And then, of course, he or she must be able to manage them. "You have to be able to keep up a positive point of view," says Don, "and you have to motivate people."

Don says his job requires him to be flexible and a problem-solver, because anything could happen, from a power failure causing the greenhouse heating system to shut down, to a beneficial suddenly losing

its appetite. A research and development manager may also have fund-raising, financial and marketing skills. Research projects usually demand a lot of investment before discoveries can be put on the market, and salaries have to be paid in the meantime.

What is
the work like?

Don's working schedule is more reasonable now that his company is firmly established. "Initially we all worked long days and weekends," he says. But even now, hours can vary enormously from one week to another. Researchers and research managers may need to come in on weekends or work nights, depending on the habits and needs of their subjects and the greenhouse environments that support them.

His work environment can vary enormously, depending on whether he is in the lab, on the road, visiting growers in the field or attending conferences.

Don does a lot of travelling, lecturing at universities and giving talks across the country to keep growers and other people in his field informed about his projects. He also talks to growers about problems they are having with pesticides. He's happy to spend a lot of time travelling because, ultimately, it gives him the opportunity to spread the word about his company's products!

►By Ingrid Phaneuf   (09/98)

AGRICULTURE

Research and Development Manager
Research and Development

■ What programme(s) I did:

B.Sc. in Entomology, University of Alberta, Alberta
M.Sc. in Entomology, University of Alberta, Alberta
B.Ed., University of Alberta, Alberta

■ Average salary
$107 610

■ What are other routes to this position?

Must have a B.Sc. and knowledge of growing systems.

■ Skills and qualities you need for this job:

- need knowledge of insects and growing systems
- must have good computer skills
- need management skills
- need fund-raising skills

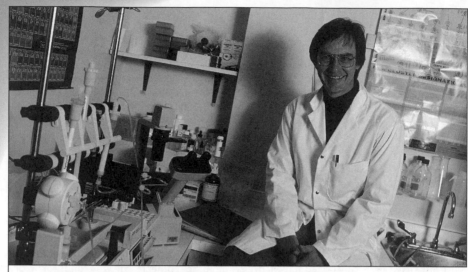

Photo : David Grandy Photography, Dartmouth

"Man of Many Hats"

In 1984, scientists discovered that by fusing normal white blood cells with cancerous blood cells, they could easily reproduce what are known as monoclonal antibodies. These are proteins which attach themselves to any foreign substances in blood like viruses or bacteria, and are useful tools in diagnosing many blood diseases.

Dominion Biologicals is one of many companies involved in making this kind of product, but unusual in that it does its research, development, manufacturing and sales on its own. The company employs only 30 people, so employees often have to wear many hats. Vice-president **Bill Eberlie** is no exception — he is research project manager and he oversees all of the company's operation.

What I do

As research project manager, Bill is responsible for co-ordinating all the research in his company's lab. The research includes finding out how effective different monoclonal antibodies are for diagnostic use, and evaluating the effectiveness of other companies' diagnostic products that are already on the market, in order to find ways to improve them. To develop a better understanding of how their own diagnostic materials work, the lab also conducts investigations of unusual red blood samples discovered by researchers using their own diagnostic materials.

Bill's job involves a lot of paperwork. He checks his employees' time sheets, supervises the payroll, writes out performance appraisals, and is directly involved in hiring staff. He also makes sure everything in the lab is in working order and purchases new equipment as needed.

Bill spends a lot of time in the lab looking over researchers' shoulders to see if their research could lead to new products or improve existing ones. "Sometimes I'll spend a day looking at unusual blood samples — just to see if they could help with our research on monoclonal antibodies," says Bill.

"We have to be able to make a product the market needs."

Along with the company president, Bill is also involved in decisions to select research projects his company will invest in. Some research projects can last as long as six years before Dominion Biologicals gets definitive results, so the company must have many projects underway at once. For Bill, this means keeping track of several projects at the same time, and spotting promising new research avenues. "A research scientist might make a new monoclonal antibody, but it means nothing until we see how we can use it," he explains. "We have to be able to make a product the market needs."

What skills
do I need?

A research project manager needs lab training and experience, first and foremost. "You could do the operations side of my job without lab experience, but not research and development," says Bill.

Bill holds a B.Sc. from the University of Western Ontario, and took post-graduate courses in management. He also holds a diploma in medical laboratory technology, and Advanced Certification in blood transfusion medicine from the Canadian Society of Laboratory Technologists.

According to Bill, computer training is essential for his work, as are a number of people skills. A research project manager has to be good with people, be able to make decisions independently, be dedicated, motivated, and be very flexible, he says.

Versatility is important. "You have to be willing to do everything, especially in a small company," he explains.

What is
the work like?

Bill works 50 to 60 hours per week. He usually starts work at 8 a.m. and finishes at around 4 p.m. But he also works weekends, and travels across Canada occasionally to explain to the company's sales representatives how the products work.

Because of travel and having to handle many research projects at once, his schedule can be fairly erratic. When Bill's not in the research lab, he's doing paperwork or meeting with researchers, the president, or other people who work for him in manufacturing and sales.

The vice-president tries to finish up paperwork first thing in the morning so he can spend the rest of the day in the lab. But because Bill has so many responsibilities related to overseeing the overall operations of the company, he often goes into the lab on weekends to look at research projects.

"I'm quite happy here," says Bill. "Even though the hours are long my job is challenging, and I learn new things every day."

▶By Ingrid Phaneuf (09/98)

HEALTH

Research Project Manager
Research and Development

■ What programme(s) I did:

B.Sc., including post-graduate courses in management, University of Western Ontario, Ontario Diploma in Medical Laboratory Technology , and Advanced Certification in blood transfusion medicine from the Canadian Society of Laboratory Technologists.

■ Average salary
$76 000

■ What are other routes to this position?

Lab training and experience and management training.

■ Skills and qualities you need for this job:

- need lab training and experience
- must have management skills
- need ability to see how research can be applied
- computer skills are essential

49

Photo : Kevin R. Bogetti-Smith, Vancouver

"The Bubble Cure"

Making sure that bubbles are all the same size may sound like child's play, but when the bubbles carry medicine inside the body, it's serious business. Just ask **Tony Nakhla**, a research scientist at Lipex Biomembranes. This firm developed the Extruder, a machine which helps form liposomes — artificial spheres which mimic cell membranes. Scientists hope that one day these liposomes will carry drugs through the body to treat diseases like cancer. This is why Tony is enthusiastic about his work. "I like the potential to devise things that are clinically applicable — things that can help people."

What I do

Tony is a Lipex Biomembranes employee, but he works in a lab at the University of British Columbia. He isn't involved in any actual experiments on drug therapies. Rather, he is working on one particular part of the process: he tests the Extruder, a stainless-steel instrument that looks like a barrel with a plate on either end. Membranes with tiny holes etched into them are inserted at the bottom and lipo-

somes are poured into the barrel. Compressed gas forces them through the membranes, creating spheres of the size needed for specific experiments or therapy.

Liposomes are spherical fats, ("lipo" means fat and "some" means spherical), which scientists make by mixing dry phospholipids - fats which mimic the substances making up much of our bodies - in water. But they are not necessarily uniform in size or shape. Tony's job is to see how different lipids and membranes react to the Extruder, so they can be made into the size and shape researchers need to target specific diseases accurately and successfully. Tony says the importance of this testing cannot be over-stated: if the liposomes don't get to the right size "they don't perform well" in the body.

Testing the Extruder is not Tony's only task. "I consult with customers and do a lot of technical support when people have problems or questions about liposomes in general. I also do a bit of marketing and I'm involved with some of the engineering."

Tony also performs co-ordination jobs for Lipex Biomembranes. The company is affiliated, through UBC, with the British Columbia Cancer Agency and with Northern Lipids, the company that formulates the lipids Lipex uses to make liposomes. Tony's job is to make this complex corporate maze simpler, by co-ordinating the efforts of these organisations, a task which involves many hours on the phone and on his computer communicating with people.

What skills
do I need?

Tony says a Ph.D. is a must for research scientists. "I talk a lot to doctors and other Ph.D.s about very specific stuff, like formulating certain vaccines, and it requires a Ph.D." Tony completed his B.Sc., M.Sc. and Ph.D., all in Biochemistry.

But besides these obvious prerequisites, he says that his job requires communications and people skills. "I go to meetings and talk to people a lot. You need to be able to answer questions and troubleshoot a lot. You have to be industrious in certain ways because we are trying to develop new products that are going to suit the market."

Tony says there is no such thing as a "regular day" for a research scientist. Research scientists typically work long hours.

When Tony started working for Lipex, he had the advantage of having already worked with the Extruder during his doctoral studies at Memorial University in Newfoundland. "My degree is in liposomes for vaccine formulations. We were using liposomes for those purposes and throughout, I was using an Extruder. So I knew a lot about the instrument."

What is
the work like?

Tony says there is no such thing as a "regular day" for a research scientist. Research scientists typically work long hours. He says he's "toned down a bit" lately, but still works between 45 and 50 hours a week, a rate which puts him on the low end of the scale in his type of work. "I think a typical research scientist would work at least 60 hours a week."

Although he works for a private company, Tony's lab is located on the University of British Columbia's campus. He considers himself lucky to be able to work in a university environment. "In an industrial environment, the stress level is higher because there's money on the line," he says.

Generally, his work takes him back and forth between his office and lab, located side by side. His lab's main equipment is an Extruder for testing, the principal part of his job. He retreats to his office to use his computer or carry out the more interpersonal aspects of his work.

▶By Christine Daviault (09/98)

HEALTH

Research Scientist 1
Research and Development

■ What programme(s) I did:

B.Sc. in Biochemistry, Concordia University, Quebec
M.Sc. in Biochemistry, Concordia University, Quebec
PhD. in Biochemistry, Memorial University, Newfoundland

■ Average salary

$62 346

■ What are other routes to this position?

A degree in a science field such as biology, chemistry or biochemistry.

■ Skills and qualities you need for this job:

- need to be a good communicator
- need strong background in science
- need to be meticulous, detail-oriented

"Born into Science"

Photo : Dawn Lane Photography, St. John's

Born in rural Newfoundland, **Sheila Drover** credits her grandmother, a teacher, for getting her interested in science. "Where I grew up, there were no doctors or nurses and it was my grandmother that people came to see when they were sick because she knew a lot about folk remedies. She taught me the importance of reading and so I read about researchers like Marie Curie, Alexander Fleming and Louis Pasteur." Sheila now does important research on rheumatoid arthritis and breast cancer. She also follows her grandmother's footsteps by teaching at Memorial University in St. John's, Newfoundland.

What I do

Sheila is an assistant professor of Immunology and a medical researcher at St. John's Faculty of Medicine. Her work involves three tasks: research — which takes up most of her time — teaching and administration.

Sheila does research on the role of histacompatibility anagens (HLA) in auto-immune diseases such as rheumatoid arthritis and breast cancer. HLA takes place when an individual's immune system, which is supposed to fight infection, starts attacking its own healthy tissues. "For reasons that we don't fully understand, some types of HLA seem to predispose an individual to the development of certain diseases or confer an increased risk for a more severe disease," says Sheila.

The HLA molecules act like bounty hunters in the immune system. They look around and trap peptides (small pieces of proteins)

from bacteria and viruses. Then they deliver these proteins to the immune system, specifically the T Cells. "The T-Cells inspect these histacompatibility molecules with the peptides and if they're foreign, for example from a virus. Then the T-Cells go right into action, they make an immune response and they actually kill the cells infected with the virus," explains Sheila.

> **"I have four students and a research assistant and part of my job is to help them design their projects and carry them through."**

In the case of breast cancer, Sheila believes that some HLA types may have a negative influence on the course of the disease. "Right now, it's almost impossible to predict the outcome for breast cancer patients who are at a very early stage of the disease. So a major focus of my work is to determine if certain HLA types can separate patients with a good prognosis - who will need no additional therapy - from those who are more likely to develop recurrence, and who could benefit from chemotherapy."

> **"In research, there are a lot of failures because your ideas don't always work out. You have to be able to stick to your goals and carry them through."**

As an assistant professor, Sheila gives two classes in immunology and supervises graduate students' work. "I have four students and a research assistant and part of my job is to help them design their projects and carry them through." Sheila also performs some administrative duties at the university, including serving on committees that decide things like hiring and curriculum.

What skills
do I need?

To succeed as a researcher, Sheila says you need to be persevering and stubborn. "In research, there are a lot of failures because your ideas don't always work out. You have to be able to stick to your goals and carry them through." Sheila says that research scientists have to be able to look at a problem and not give up until they find a solution.

Scientific curiosity and dedication are at the top of Sheila's list of essential qualities. Manual dexterity is also a bonus, she says, since the type of work she is doing involves a lot of precision.

As for formal training, Sheila believes that, when possible, a degree in biotechnology is the best preparation for a research scientist working in the industry. If that's not possible, then she suggests a degree in either biochemistry or biology. A Ph.D. is essential nowadays to work as a researcher.

What is
the work like?

Sheila's work takes place in two different labs at Memorial University; one where she grows cells for use in experiments, and another, the DNA lab, where she and her staff work on isolating and identifying the different types of HLA.

Sheila's schedule is definitely not 9 to 5. She works at least 10 hours every day, much of it in the laboratory, bathed in fluorescent light and surrounded by beakers, droppers, glass dishes and microscopes. Long hours are not a problem for Sheila. "To be a medical researcher, you need to be totally committed. It takes up every day of the week, and almost all your waking hours. You don't do this as a job, but because you truly love it, because you want to try and make a difference and because really do want to discover something. "

▶By Christine Daviault   (09/98)

HEALTH

Research Scientist 2
Research and Development

■ What programme(s) I did:

Diploma of Medical Laboratory Technology, College of the North Atlantic, Newfoundland
Diploma, Registered Medical Laboratory Technologist, Canadian Society of Medical Technologists, Ontario
Diploma, Advanced Registered Technologist, Canadian Society of Medical Technologists, Ontario
M.Sc. in Immunology, Memorial University, Newfoundland
Ph.D. in Immunology, Memorial University, Newfoundland

■ Average salary

$54 329

■ What are other routes to this position?

B.Sc. in Biochemistry, Biology or Biotechnology.

■ Skills and qualities you need for this position:

- need to be curious
- should enjoy manual tasks
- need patience and perseverance

Photo : McMaster Photographers, Saskatoon

"The Plant Healer"

Rakesh Kapoor has always been a firm believer in the power of plants to maintain good health, and to prevent and cure many ailments. His job as a research scientist at Bioriginal Food and Science Corp., a Saskatchewan company specialising in the production of essential oils and organic crops, gives him the chance to prove this and work in a field that fascinates him. "What I like most about this job is that I learn something new every day," he says.

What I do

Rakesh is a research scientist who works as manager of new products at Bioriginal Inc., a company with 50 employees that produces neutraceuticals — medicinal products made from herbs or other natural sources. Rakesh, who has a Ph.D. in Physiology, is responsible for the scientific research and development at Bioriginal. Drawing on his extensive knowledge of plants, he reads scientific research on medicinal plants and tries to come up with new formulations for the company's line of essential oils, which include Borage, Evening Primrose, Flax and Pumpkin oils.

To be specific, Rakesh is looking for new ways to put essential oils to work. It's a bit like improving on your grandmother's recipes, he says. You start with an existing product, or recipe, and add a certain herb or combine different oils to achieve different results. He has already found new nutritional supplements which combine the company's oils, as a source of essential fatty acids, with some vitamins and herbs. "These capsules can be taken to prevent certain diseases or to maintain good health," he says. Rakesh is also studying the effect of the oil of an herb called Borage on the relief of inflammatory conditions, such as arthritis.

According to Rakesh, a good research scientist needs an analytical mind and a critical eye.

Rakesh is also responsible for supervising and co-ordinating clinical trials at Bioriginal. He thinks of new possible research avenues, finds researchers to do the trials, designs protocols, and evaluates their progress. "There are a number of challenges involved in conducting trials. You have to find research groups willing to work on dietary supplements without expecting too much money." This, he says, is not as obvious as it may seem. "We're not a pharmaceutical company so we can't spend a million dollars on trials or patent our products. We can prove that the carrot is good for your eyesight, but we can't patent the carrot." He says that companies are slowly becoming more interested in dietary supplements.

What skills
do I need?

Rakesh completed a B.Sc. in Pharmacy in India, where he worked five years in the pharmaceutical industry, and a Ph.D. with a specialisation in Cardiovascular Physiology in Saskatechewan. He says that a background in nutrition or food sciences is important for his job, as well as a good knowledge of plants and their impact on our health.

"If you're not willing to spend a few hours a day reading, you'll never do it."

According to Rakesh, a good research scientist needs an analytical mind and a critical eye. "You can't believe a statement at face value, you have to analyse the rationale behind it," he says. Rakesh says it's also important to be passionate about research, especially when the rewards for your hard work may not come in the short-term. He

says scientists must be driven by curiosity, and not rewards, because it can take many years of hard work before the rewards come.

Rakesh also says that being a good research scientist calls for good reading habits. "It's very important," he says, both to stay up to date in your area of interest and to know what other scientists are up to. "If you're not willing to spend a few hours a day reading, you'll never do it."

What is
the work like?

Bioriginal's main offices are located in Innovation Place, an agricultural biotech centre on the University of Saskatchewan campus. This centre has been recognised by the United Nations as one of the top five agricultural research facilities in the world. Rakesh works there most of the time, except when he travels to the various research labs across Saskatchewan doing work for Bioriginal.

Research is a field demanding long hours of work. Rakesh sometimes works as many as 12 or 15 hours a day, sometimes seven days a week. When he's done at the office, he goes home and spends another three hours catching up on his reading. His long hours are a sign of his passion for his work.

▶By Christine Daviault   (09/98)

HEALTH

Research Scientist 3
Research and Development

■ What programme(s) I did:

B.Sc. in Pharmacy, University of Delhi, India
M.Sc. Pharmacognosy, University of Delhi, India
Ph.D. in Physiology, specialisation in Cardiovascular Physiology, U. of Saskatchewan , Saskatchewan

■ Average salary

$49 218

■ What are other routes to this position?

A degree in Pharmacognosy or a degree in Nutritional Science.

■ Skills and qualities you need for this job:

- need strong analytical skills
- should be willing to work long hours
- need to be curious

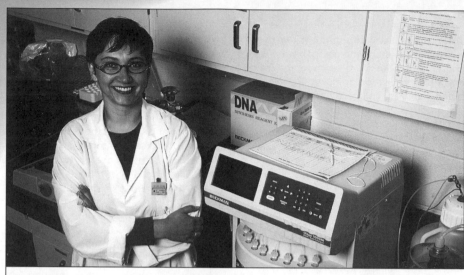

Photo : Kevin R. Bogetti-Smith, Vancouver

"Stefanie to the Rescue"

Stefanie Butland is a research technician at the plant biochemistry laboratory in the University of British Columbia's Faculty of Agricultural Sciences. Scientists in the lab where Butland works study plants and what's inside them: DNA, molecules, enzymes and genes. When Stefanie is working directly on the research being performed in the lab, she works for the professor who is running the research. But while she is performing her other job - supervising everybody else while they are using the lab's equipment -Stefanie is in charge!

What I do

As a research technician, Stefanie has to show people who use the lab (there are about 10) how to use the equipment. Laboratory equipment can be pretty complex — and in the field of biochemistry, like all sciences, it is getting more sophisticated and hi-tech every day. In Stefanie's experience, even Ph.D. students need someone to explain how the machinery works! In her supervisory role, Stefanie also helps her colleagues with research problems, opens

mail, and generally keeps the lab running smoothly.

Stefanie also comes up with her own ideas for research, and if her boss feels her ideas can contribute to the research that's already going on, he'll let her go ahead with it.

Despite these responsibilities, Stefanie manages to find time to do research herself. "My dream day is getting to spend all day in front of the computer, even lunch, comparing DNA sequences using Web tools," she says. Research projects are collaborative efforts between various scientists with different skills, and comparing DNA sequences is just one of the tasks involved. One of the projects at the plant biochemistry lab is to find a way to prevent mould growing on strawberries before they're picked. Stefanie's role in the project is to see if genes from fungus-resistant plants can be added to the strawberry plant's genetic make-up to help it resist the fungus.

Another research project the lab recently worked on was developing trees with less lignan, a substance that requires toxic chemicals for its removal. Making trees with less lignan would make the pulp-and-paper industry less harmful to the environment. Stefanie's role in the project was to study the genes that make the lignan itself, and the different plants that contain it.

Stefanie also comes up with her own ideas for research, and if her boss feels her ideas can contribute to the research that's already going on, he'll let her go ahead with it.

What skills
do I need?

Stefanie has an M.Sc. in Biology, with a specialty in Molecular Biology. Getting the M.Sc. was important, she says, because it exposed her to different research techniques. Knowing a lot of research techniques comes in handy in the lab, where Stefanie spends a lot of time helping other researchers. The research technician has to be able to share her knowledge of how equipment works, and how to approach research problems.

Computer skills are an absolute necessity to Stefanie's job. So are mastery of the scientific method, and a good memory.

She must also be able to work in an environment in which she is frequently interrupted and her attention is divided among different people's work. Like everyone in a lab, Stefanie must also be able to adapt

quickly to change. If a research project isn't producing results, researchers have to be ready to try a new approach, or start a completely different project, sometimes without much notice.

According to Stefanie, the job of research technician all boils down to being able to work in a team. "A lot of people think scientists work alone in closets," she says. "It's not true. The best scientists are outgoing and like to collaborate."

What is
the work like?

Stefanie works 9 a.m. to 5 p.m. most days. Because she supervises the use of the lab, she generally has to be at work early, between 9 and 9:30 am. She usually works a normal 40-hour week, but that can vary. If plants being used for research need weekend waterings, she goes in and waters them.

Laboratories are not exactly calm, orderly places. The environment at the plant biochemistry lab is never quiet and there are many things going on at once. A research technician is constantly interrupted and asked questions.

Stefanie also shares her office, which is near the lab, with three other people. "If I want quiet time to think about my research, I have to go to the library," she says.

▶By Ingrid Phaneuf   (09/98)

AGRICULTURE

Research Technician

Research and Development

■ What programme(s) I did:

B.Sc., York University, Ontario
M.Sc. in Biology: speciality in Molecular Biology, York University, Ontario

■ Average salary

$36 488

■ What are other routes to this position?

Must have B.Sc. and should have M.Sc., preferably in the field the lab is working in.

■ Skills and qualities you need for this job:

- need computer skills
- need knowledge of scientific method and research tools
- should be good communicator and networker
- need good time-management skills

"The Road to a Cancer Block"

Photo : Courtesy of Laboratoiries AETERNA

Tropical medicine seems an unlikely background for work in Quebec. But it led **Marc Rivière** to become Vice-President of Clinical Affairs at AEterna Laboratories, a Quebec City company that might be on the verge of creating a new, possibly revolutionary, cancer treatment.

What I do

As Vice-President of Clinical Affairs, Marc manages the department of clinical research at AEterna, whose main project at the moment is Neovastat, a new anti-cancer drug. Neovastat is made from cells found in shark cartilage, and seems to block the formation of blood vessels in cancerous tumours. Without new blood vessels, tumours can't grow. Neovastat won't cure cancer, but will block tumours from progressing, keeping patients alive longer.

The drug has shown a lot of potential in pre-clinical trials (tests on animals). It has none of the side effects typically associated with chemotherapy. But there's more. AE-941 — official name for the group of cells Neovastat is made from — has also proven effective against other conditions aggravated by blood cell growth, including the skin condition psoriasis. If Neovastat passes the clinical trial stage, where it is tested on humans, it could revolutionize the treatment of cancer and many chronic diseases.

Marc's work involves three main aspects. As vice-president, he is responsible for meeting with financial analysts to convince them of AEterna's and Neovastat's value. He also gives presentations on AEterna's clinical test results at conferences, and sees the people in his department have all the necessary resources to do their work, by allocating money and resources to the different members of his team.

Marc believes that in order to enjoy biotechnology work, particularly in small companies, you must like risk.

Marc also directs clinical research at AEterna, collecting information and speaking to experts to decide what clinical studies AEterna will conduct— whether to test a certain drug for its effect on lung or prostate cancer, for example. Then he writes a protocol, a sort of a guide book on how the study should be conducted. Before he asks doctors to do the actual testing, he must get government authorisations for the study. "The complete process can take up to two and a half years," he says.

Finally, Marc does management duties, which includes recruiting new staff – he has hired ten people since he joined AEterna a year ago – doing employee evaluations and interacting with other departments. He works closely with the pre-clinical research department to orient AEterna's research. "If a doctor conducting a clinical study on cancer observes that our product has a particular effect on the patient, we might ask the pre-clinical research department to do in-vivo experiments on rats to try to understand why."

What skills
do I need?
Marc believes that in order to enjoy biotechnology work, particularly in small companies, you must like risk. Companies must invest millions of dollars in research on products which may not get to the market. To work in such an atmosphere, you must live with stress. Marc says this aspect of his job is not necessarily a drawback. "You get a much broader experience. It's more interesting and less repetitive."

Marc doesn't believe you need a string of degrees to succeed as Director of clinical research. "I think experience makes the difference. Young people should pursue their studies as far as they can but must be aware that degrees are not everything. They help,

but they'll never replace experience." What you need, he says, is an open mind, passion and good intuition. To get experience, he suggests internships in the biotechnology industry.

What is
the work like?
Unlike many biotech companies, AEterna finances its research and development with the sales of other products derived from its research, including facial creams and dietary supplements. At the end of 1998, the company will be moving into a brand-new, larger building near Quebec City to house its growing personnel.

While his official office hours are from 8 to 5, Marc says his schedule depends on his workload. However, he doesn't like to stay at the office too late, so he often takes his laptop computer home to finish work.

Marc also attends conferences where he might present the latest clinical research results on one of the company's products. For example, he recently attended a congress in Stockholm, Sweden, where he presented clinical test results for drugs to treat lung and prostate cancers. "I go to about 10 congresses a year and try to send people in my team to two congresses per year," he concludes. If Neovastat succeeds in its clinical trials, Marc will be attending even more!

►By Christine Daviault   (09/98)

HEALTH

Senior Research Executive
Research and Development

■ What programme(s) I did:
Doctorate in Medicine (MD), Paul Sabatier University, France
Specialisation in Tropical Medicine, University of Bordeaux II, France

■ Average salary
$132 953

■ What are other routes to this position?
Science background with some management experience or vice-versa.

■ Skills and qualities you need for this job:
- need good communication skills
- need problem-solving skills
- must be bilingual (French/English in Quebec and English/Spanish in the U.S.A.)
- need working knowledge of word processing software

59

Photo : Daniels & Glionna Photography, Toronto

"Creating LIFE"

As University of Toronto professor **Michael Sefton** lay in bed one sleepless night, a thought came to him. What if he were to convince a group of scientists and researchers to work together to make a tissue-engineered heart, a device that would look, act and function just like a real heart? So began the LIFE (Living Implants from Engineering) project which brings together 13 specialists from around the world to create the new heart as well as other replacement organs like kidneys and livers.

What I do

As the founder of LIFE, Michael met with the other members and developed a plan for creating the tissue-engineered heart. Tissue engineering currently involves either planting special cells in the body to make something like new skin grow or implanting a human-made material in the body to make something happen (make a blood vessel grow for example). Michael says the heart project will probably take about 10 years, adding "It's a challenge. We're pushing the limit of what we can do."

The LIFE project is only one of Michael's jobs as a professor in the Department of Chemical Engineering and Applied Chemistry. He also teaches chemical engineering, which uses chemistry either to solve problems in the production of chemicals (for example, creating plastics or pharmaceutical products) or to create new materials like the tissue-engineered heart.

> **"It's not just enough to write a paper and then forget about the work. I'd like to see the work out there helping the patients."**

Michael estimates he spends about five hours in the classroom each week. He teaches both undergraduates and graduate students working towards a Master's degree or a Ph.D. Because he's been teaching for 25 years, he says it takes him about three hours each week to prepare his lecture notes. "But it's a lot more when I'm teaching a course that I've never taught before," he says.

Research and writing up the research results for publication in science journals is another part of his work. Projects like LIFE come under the research side. Michael says its important to him that results from experiments and research he does at the University move beyond the campus walls into the real world. "It's not just enough to write a paper and then forget about the work," he says. " I'd like to see the work out there helping the patients."

What skills
do I need?

"I don't think everyone is cut out to be a professor," Michael says. "People need to be a bit idiosyncratic to do this job." Professors have a varied set of skills and qualities starting with a love of teaching and an interest in doing scientific research. Although Michael spends just five hours a week in the classroom, most of his day is spent talking with students, showing them how to conduct their own experiments and answering their questions. "You have to be able to listen and to communicate clearly," he says.

The job also demands a great deal of creativity, Michael adds. Professors themselves, and not some outside person, determine the critical problems or issues in their field and how to go about solving them.

Nowadays, professors often collaborate on experiments with other researchers or with private companies. Sharing work requires "a sense of humour and an element of modesty," Michael says. In the engi-neering field, most professors work regularly with private companies, he adds, because those companies are willing to fund engineering research in hopes that the experiments will produce something that ultimately can be sold to the public.

What is
the work like?

People often think being a university professor is a cushy job, Michael says. They especially think professors get the summer off. Not so. "We work all year round, just like other people," he says. During the school year, professors spend more time teaching and working with students. In the summer, they work more closely with graduate students, do their research and write.

Michael usually arrives on campus about 9:30 a.m. and doesn't leave until 5:30 p.m. He's rarely alone in his office as students and other professors come in to discuss their work. To find the quiet time he needs to write, Michael usually takes a portable computer home with him and works there. He also uses his commute time on the Toronto subway to read science journals and papers.

The long hours are all worth it, Michael says. After 25 years as a professor, he still loves his job. "I get to set my own agenda," he says. "I get to do what I want to do. I'm essentially my own boss. "

▶By Liz Warwick   (09/98)

HEALTH

University Professor
Research and Development

■ What programme(s) I did:

B.Sc. in Chemical Engineering, University of Toronto, Ontario
Ph.D. in Chemical Engineering, Massachusetts Institute of Technology, U.S.A.

■ Average salary

$67 868

■ What are other routes to this position?

To be a professor, you need a Ph.D. in your field (chemical engineering, chemistry, biology, etc.).

■ Skills and qualities you need for this job:

- must be able to teach and work with students
- must have excellent communication skills
- must like setting own agenda and following through
- must be willing to take risks

"The Test Tube Calf"

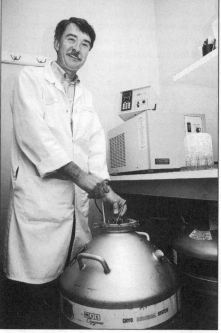

Photo : PPM, Montreal

Reproduction technology has always fascinated **Daniel Bousquet**. "It's amazing to be able to create a new being, to manipulate life." Trained as a veterinarian, he now works as Director of Research and Development for L'Alliance Boviteq, a small company specialising in bovine reproduction.

What I do

Daniel works at a research centre near Montreal, in St-Hyacinthe. This town is the home of the University of Montreal's Faculty of Veterinary Medecine where ground-breaking animal research is done. The 18 Alliance Boviteq employees identify and remove eggs from cows with specific genetic characteristics, like high milk production. They use these to develop embryos for resale.

Daniel divides his time between lab and managerial work. He likes the combination of tasks.

Daniel's job is to see that the embryos meet customers' criteria. These fall into two categories: embryos with genes for high milk production or better meat, and gender choice. "Milk producers, for example, are more interested in females, while meat producers prefer male animals," explains Daniel.

The parents' pedigree determines their genetic qualities. According to the bull and cow's track record (quantity of milk produced or percentage of successful pregnancies), Daniel evaluates statistically what the chances are of obtaining the desired genetic make-up. These "super" cows can cost as much as $100 000 on the market. To find such animals, L'Alliance Boviteq sends representatives to fairs across North America where breeders bring their most prized animals.

In the lab, Daniel removes eggs from the cow's ovaries and places them in a petri dish with the bull's sperm for 18 hours to be fertilised. The fertilised eggs are then placed in an environment similar to a cow's uterus for seven days. During this time the embryo grows from one cell to between 150 and 200 cells. At this point, it's easy to determine the embryo's sex and the best time to freeze it for resale.

"You have to like reading scientific journals and always be willing to recycle your knowledge. We're always studying."

Daniel divides his time between lab and managerial work. He meets with employees weekly to help them plan their work, and with the two other directors to plan company management. He likes the combination of tasks. "It takes a balance between the two. It's obvious that lab work is fascinating because that's when we get to verify our hypotheses. But without planning, the work wouldn't result in anything."

Most of the firm's clients are Quebec and international milk producers. "We do business with twenty countries throughout the world, in Spain, and in South America, who want Canadian genetic characteristics for their cattle. Our milk cattle's genetic make-up is considered the world's best". Embryos are sent in a tank filled with liquid nitrogen. One such tank can contain up to I 000 embryos and bring $500 000 on the market, each embryo selling for an average $500.

What skills
do I need?
Daniel knew early on he wanted to work in the bovine reproduction field. "It's almost a calling. You need to have a long-term outlook. The rest can be developed during your training."

Daniel completed a B.Sc. in veterinary medicine, a M.Sc. in reproduction and clinical sciences and a Ph.D. in reproduction physiology. He believes success in his field comes from a passion for research. "You must really have a taste for it. You have to like research. If you don't, you might become a technician, but today, we need people who can solve problems."

You also have to love studies, because acquiring the skills you need for this job

entails a lot of time hitting the books. "You have to like reading scientific journals and always be willing to recycle your knowledge. We're always studying." To do his job, Daniel says you need scientific and general curiosity, but also patience and flexibility.

What is
the work like?
Daniel begins a typical day looking at his email. "I belong to an international network of researchers working on embryos and fertilisation. We ask questions, provide answers and exchange information. For example, someone might have discovered a new recipe, another might be wondering how to perform a specific manipulation."

Lab supervision is his next job. "I go to the lab every day to make sure everything is working well. If it is, I go back to my office where I get down to the other part of my work, writing reports and answering mail."

In addition to his daily duties, Daniel stays in touch with new developments in the field of bovine reproduction by attending or organising conferences. "Next week I have to give a speech in Vancouver on reproduction biotechnologies. I'm also in charge of the scientific component of a congress to be held in St-Hyacinthe this Fall. I see it as a form of continuing education."

▶By Christine Daviault   (09/98)

AGRICULTURE

Veterinarian
Research and Development

■ What programme(s) I did:
B.Sc. in Veterinary Medicine, University of Montreal's Faculty of Veterinary Medicine in St-Hyacinthe, Quebec
M.Sc. in Reproduction and Clinical Sciences, University of Montreal's Faculty of Veterinary Medicine in St-Hyacinthe, Quebec
Ph.D. in Physiology of Reproduction, University of Montreal Faculty of Medicine, Quebec
Post-doctoral studies in in-vitro fertilisation, University of Pennsylvania in Pennsylvania, U.S.A.

■ Average salary
$76 158

■ What are other routes to this position?
B.Sc. in Biology or in Agronomy.

■ Skills and qualities you need for this job:
- must have basic computer skills
- should be curious, flexible and patient
- need to be able to work with others
- need to be bilingual

Photo : Kevin R. Bogetti-Smith, Vancouver

"Chemical Care"

Jon Barna works for a company that makes fats, waxes, oils and other lipids, substances used in a variety of biomedical products including coating liquid for capsules. Lipids are stored in chemicals such as chloroform, ether and benzene. As director of technical operations, Jon's job is to make sure that the 300 potentially hazardous chemicals are handled, stored and shipped properly and don't cause any accidents at his company. In short, he makes sure employees are safe, regulators are happy and clients obtain high-quality products.

What I do

Jon doesn't work with these chemicals themselves. His job is to ensure that every step in the manufacturing process is conducted safely, properly and consistently. To do this, Jon has to put two safety systems in place, one to make sure that standard operating procedures (called SOPs) involving chemicals are being followed, and another to keep track of which chemicals the company has, where they are being stored, and in what quantity.

Jon writes and maintains an SOP for each of the 33 operations carried out in the Northern Lipids lab. The SOP stipulates the steps in a technical operation so that all technicians work in precisely the same way. Even simple operations — like setting balances used for measuring chemicals — are documented in precise detail. To make sure technicians don't forget the steps in each procedure, Jon tests them at least once a month, and he regularly reviews the SOPs to make sure they remain up to date and complete.

The chemical tracking system, which Jon recently computerised, registers the location and quantity of any chemicals on site. It also locates the material safety data sheet and any hazards, precautions, or disposal concerns to be considered handling the chemical. Employees log the shipment, use and disposal of chemicals on a regular basis. Jon also conducts quality assurance safety inspections every month to check all procedures, devices and controls. If anything strikes him as inaccurate or unusual —like a problem with the digital environmental control systems monitoring temperature in the facility, or a problem with a fume hood in the ventilation system — he deals with it right away. Jon also "chases paper for other people," he says. "People are very busy here and sometimes forget to sign or fill out something. It's my job is to follow up and make sure that everything has been completed the way it should have been."

What skills
do I need?

One of Jon's most important aptitudes is attention to detail: in his eight months at Northern Lipids Inc, this quality has propelled him from a marketing sales position to director of technical operations.

Jon is a biophysicist by training, but had acquired considerable administrative experience before starting work at Northern Lipids. He spent 18 years working in the pharmaceutical industry for companies such as Wyeth-Ayerst, Smith Kline Beecham, Hoechst Marion Roussel and Schering, first as a research technician, then in the quality assurance department and later in research and development. He then spent almost 12 years running his own business renovating heritage buildings in Ontario.

All of these different jobs gave Jon experience in marketing, dealing with regulatory boards, and "general knowledge of how things work" — all of which are crucial to his present job.

Jon says practical hands-on laboratory skills are also essential for his work. These include general scientific techniques such as preparing buffers, tissue cultures, and experimental protein anti-body binding. "As an undergraduate, I got my first job over 13 other graduates just on the basis that I had 3 000 hours of lab work and they didn't" he says. "Never underrate the importance of practical training."

What is
the work like?

Although he doesn't have fixed hours, Jon is always in his office between 9 a.m. and 5 p.m. but sometimes works from 8 a.m. until 7 p.m. and on Saturdays. He usually wears slacks and a shirt to work, or jeans when he wants to test SOPs in the lab.

He begins each day looking at email and faxes. Then he chooses a specific project for the day: a safety inspection, SOP overview or upgrading of the quality control systems. He also spends a lot of his time on the computer checking paperwork and writing reports.

Northern Lipids occupies the top floor of the Jack Bell Research Centre, affiliated with the Vancouver General Health Science Hospital. Jon spends a good part of his day wandering through the office looking for certificates of analysis, shipping or receiving documents, or checking equipment. That's his job: making sure "everything is where it's supposed to be and everything is filed and cross-referenced."

▶By Tracey Arial   (09/98)

HEALTH

Biochemical Development
Quality Control

■ What programme(s) I did:

B.Sc., Sir George Williams University (now Concordia University), Quebec.
M.Sc. in Biophysics from McGill University, Quebec.

■ Average salary

$46 000

■ What are other routes to this position?

Any scientific training combined with pharmaceutical or biotechnology administration experience.

■ Skills and qualities you need for this job:

- must be detail-oriented
- need training in administration and regulatory affairs
- must be able to motivate people
- should be interested in technology

65

Photo : Kevin R. Bogetti-Smith, Vancouver

"Saving Lives with Statistics"

As a biostatician with the Canadian HIV Trials network, **Anona Thorne** collects, analyses, interprets and presents statistics on people who participate in HIV/AIDS treatment studies. Her work then provides drug companies and doctors information they need to treat patients with HIV or AIDS more effectively. "The fact that this is a socially worthwhile thing to do makes it that much more satisfying for me," she says.

What I do

The Canadian HIV Trials Network is a federally-funded, non-profit organisation set up to help researchers run HIV/AIDS studies and share their results. It is run jointly by the University of British Columbia (UBC) and St. Paul's Hospital in Vancouver. Anona was hired to analyse findings of HIV and AIDS studies throughout Canada.

Using a computer software which compiles data, Anona analyses information to determine how well a treatment worked and what the side-effects were. Afterwards, she works on journal articles about these studies so doctors, drug manufacturers and

other researchers can learn more about HIV and AIDS treatment.

Anona is also working on a computer simulation of the AIDS epidemic in Vancouver's downtown East Side. The programme, which has a virtual population of 10 000, was created to predict how the epidemic will unfold and the likely impact of specific treatments such as needle exchange programmes. Anona provides each virtual citizen with a theoretical HIV status and programs the software with the statistical likelihood of the disease being passed from one citizen to another when they share needles. She compiles her simulation with random needle sharing and matches the results to the actual incidence rate of the edpidemic. So far, she has successfully duplicated the epidemic from the early 80s, when it started, until 1997.

Anona's strong computer background has enabled her to take on other projects at UBC. She develops, organises, collects and documents the software used by all biostaticians working for the network, UBC and St. Paul's Hospital. She also decides which new software to purchase and trains her colleagues on it. And she'll soon begin teaching a graduate course in statistics for the Health Care and Epidemiology department.

What skills
do I need?

Anona has always liked analytical work. Although she spent years working in data processing, payroll and computer consulting, she always knew she would eventually go back to school to study math. She finally got to do it just before turning 39.

After her undergraduate degree, Anona didn't know where her education would lead. When her programme advisor suggested statistics, she balked. "I didn't know a lot about what statisticians actually do and I think I had the same impression as many people, that they work for Statistics Canada figuring out how many people live in Saskatoon and what their average income is."

Her opinion soon changed. Statisticians find openings in almost every industry these days. "Everyone who graduates with a master's in statistics finds a job quite easily," says Anona. "When I was finishing my Master's, several organisations visited the department wondering if anybody would be graduating soon."

Anona decided to work in biostatistics simply because the job offer at UBC appealed to her. She had no particular background in medicine, and her job doesn't really require one. "The nice thing about statistics is that you can work in a number of different kinds of fields," she says. "Each time you work in a slightly different field you get to learn about what is going on there." Her own work requires strong mathematical and analytical skills, as well as organisation and communications skills.

What is
the work like?

Anona works Sunday to Thursday, from 7 a.m. until 3 p.m. She likes to avoid commuter traffic and working early hours also gives her uninterrupted time and lets her avoid working late at night.

The first thing she does when she gets to the office is check and respond to email. Then she works on whatever project she's decided will be the major focus that day. Right now, Anona is preparing the course outline for a basic introductory statistics course she is planning to give in the fall. "This is the first time I'm teaching it, so I want to get it all prepared before the course actually starts."

At other times, Anona talks with other statisticians, reads publications about new statistical techniques or new HIV/AIDS treatments, or writes reports. Most of the time, though, you'll find her using her computer, calculating and plotting results or finding an interpretation for them, and using her statistical knowledge to fight the scourge of AIDS.

▶By Tracey Arial   (09/08)

HEALTH

Biostatistician
Clinical Research

■ What programme(s) I did:

B.A in Mathematics, University of British Columbia, British Columbia
M.Sc. in Statistics, University of British Columbia, British Columbia

■ Average salary

$53 452

■ What are other routes to this position ?

Bachelor's degree in Statistics or Master's degree in Statistics.

■ Skills and qualities you need for this job:

- need analytical and writing skills
- must have organisational skills
- need project management experience
- must know statistical methodology for biomedical research

67

"Bringing Business East"

Photo : David Grandy Photography, Dartmouth

When several teaching hospitals and medical schools in Eastern Canada set up Clinical Trials Atlantic Corporation (CTAC), they had one goal: to encourage major drug companies from Toronto, Montreal and the United States to test their drugs in the Atlantic provinces, providing work for researchers in the East. **Paula Jones-Wright**, a former nurse, former teacher and avid researcher, makes sure it happens. Her job is part public relations spokesperson, part seminar organiser, part auditor and part educator.

What I do

Clinical research refers to the stage of drug development when medication is actually tested on humans. It typically takes many years of research and development, or R&D, before pharmaceutical companies get to this stage. As Clinical Research Associate at the non-profit CTAC , Paula's principal task is to get to know every clinical researcher in Atlantic Canada. This enables her to recommend specific Maritime researchers to CEOs and hospital boards requesting her help.

Paula combines an active work schedule with her role as the mother of three children under five, so it's not surprising she considers being well-organised her most important professional skill!

This task calls for innovative means of promoting Atlantic expertise. Paula recently helped CTAC organise an educational symposium on clinical research which brought drug company officials to Halifax to meet with local researchers. Two hundred people from across Canada attended.

Paula is an expert in Good Research Practice (GRP), a set of rules (recently approved by the World Health Organisation) ensuring that researchers treat human subjects ethically. In particular, GRP rules specify that people on whom drugs are tested know exactly what is being studied, and how the tests will be conducted. For instance, research subjects must sign a consent form describing the study and attesting that they understand it, before any tests begin. The rules ensure that all lab processes are double-checked and each step in the trials is recorded, as is the procedure followed to arrive at specific results. As a Clinical Research Associate, Paula audits researchers to make sure they follow GRP.

As part of her job, Paula also trains other CRAs and Clinical Research Coordinators. This means she frequently travels to major cities across the country.

What skills do I need?

Paula combines an active work schedule with her role as the mother of three children under five, so it's not surprising she considers being well-organised her most important professional skill! Still, her interest in research, and the skills she has picked up in her field, are central to her work.

Paula first became interested in research as a nursing student at Dalhousie University. "I took a course that involved a lot of research at the undergraduate level and then went on to do research at the Masters' level, mainly in education." After her studies, Paula worked as a research coordinator in a labour delivery unit. That is where she developed a specialisation in clinical trials.

Paula never thought she'd leave her job at Dalhousie. She had even been mentioned in the prestigious New England Journal of Medicine for her success in recruiting patients for one of her projects. However, when the CTAC position opened up, she says, "it seemed to describe my skills perfectly", namely an in-depth knowledge of clinical research. "Physicians I worked with encouraged me to apply."

What is
the work like?
Most days for Paula begin at 8:30. After dropping the children off at the nearby university-run day-care centre, she goes through voice mail and email at her office. Then she touches base with other CTAC employees to brainstorm on ideas and projects underway. "We want to act on as many new ideas as possible" she says.

After this discussion, Paula gets down to what she calls her daily "grind". She might interview researchers. She might go through paperwork, such as consent forms or budgets. She might send out thank-you notes and cheques to speakers who participated in special events. She might design course curricula.

"This is not a routine job."

Sometimes, a single message or email determines Paula's activities for an entire day, especially if someone is seeking researchers in the Atlantic region. A local hospital wanting to set up new research might ask her to pass on new studies. An international pharmaceutical company might want to fund a researcher. She's thrilled to help.

Most days end at 5:30, unless Paula has to travel to another city to give a course or she decides to work on her own research. "This is not a routine job," says Paula. "There's never been a day when I've done the same thing."

▶By Tracey Arial   (09/98)

HEALTH

Clinical Research Associate
Clinical Research

■ What programme(s) I did:

B.Sc. in Nursing, Dalhousie University, Nova Scotia
ICU Nurse, I.W.K. Grace Health Centre, Nova Scotia
B.Ed., St. Mary's University, Nova Scotia
M.Ed. Adult Education, St. Mary's University, Nova Scotia

■ Average salary

$58 438

■ What are other routes to this position?

Clinical Research Coordinators usually begin as nurses, and usually have a Masters' degree in Science.

■ Skills and qualities you need for this job:

- need organisation skills
- need research experience
- must have teaching experience

69

"On the Genetic Trail"

Photo : PPM, Montreal

Algène Biotechnologies is a research company that specialises in the study of diseases believed to be hereditary. These include Alzheimer's disease, schizophrenia, Parkinson's disease and even migraine headaches. However, in order to find the genetic trails that might explain how a disease occurs, Algène needs to get its hands on actual genetic material from individual people. Algène often studies families where these diseases occur frequently. That's where **Claudine Giguère** comes in. As field co-ordinator for Algène, she looks for subjects in specific regions who are willing to donate blood, and teams of nurses willing to extract it, and she makes sure these "field" operations unfold without a hitch.

What I do

When research scientists at Algène decide they want to study a particular disease, their first job is to decide is to pick a region in Quebec in which to conduct it. They might, for example, look for a population which decends from a very small number of founders (important in studying difference between specific genes).

A project takes at least two years from beginning to end, with any number of field studies and pauses in between.

Claudine's job starts after the main decisions about the orientation of the project have been made. Her first task is to participate in the writing of description of the project and the tests. The project is then sent to the ethics committee of the hospital where the tests will be administered. The committee determines whether the research project's value justifies asking subjects to donate their time and blood, and gives Algène permission to conduct the study.

If the ethics committee has questions about the research project, Claudine answers them. If they want changes on the project, she makes sure they are made. Once the project is cleared, Claudine begins contacting doctors in the project area to ask them to refer patients willing to participate in the project. "Most people are willing," says Claudine, "either because they already have the disease we're studying, or because their children are at risk of developing it. They have a personal interest in advancing the research." (Subjects are not paid for participation, but are compensated for any expenses incurred travelling or missing a day of work.)

Claudine also sets up networks of nurses in areas where studies are being conducted. The nurses travel to subjects' homes to draw blood or help them fill out questionnaires. For complicated tests requiring medical assessment, like neurological exams, the subjects travel to local clinics. In either case, Claudine is responsible for making sure the people conducting the tests do so correctly. She travels to the region under study to train nurses for the project, then does follow-up over the phone.

Claudine also has to make sure all the test results, questionnaires, and blood samples get back to the lab. A project takes at least two years from beginning to end, with any number of field studies and pauses in between. "A project is carried out in several stages. It can stop for a few months, and then start up again for any number of reasons. Sometimes the researchers want to start tests all over again because the initial results were inconclusive, or the samples were unusable." Claudine usually works on several projects at the same time.

What skills
do I need?

A field coordinator definitely needs writing and communications skills, and a good understanding of the scientific method. Claudine writes the protocol (test procedures) for nurses conducting the tests, and makes sure these nurses understand and

are able to follow protocol. She often has to meet with them and train them.

Claudine also works with company statisticians to make sure the wording of questionnaires for subjects is just right, and that there are no misunderstandings of the questions being asked.

"During a rush period I can work as much as 80 hours in one week."

An understanding of bio-ethics is also essential for writing project proposals for ethics committee consultations. "Ethics committees often request more information about our projects because of their genetic nature," explains Claudine. "They're a little afraid of what we're doing."

What the
work is like?

Claudine works about 40 hours per week, or more if she needs to travel or is working on a tight deadline. "During a rush period I can work as much as 80 hours in one week," she says.

When Claudine doesn't have to travel to train personnel or attend conventions on bio-ethics, she works in her office. The atmosphere there can vary from peaceful to hectic. "During a rush period, the phone just doesn't stop ringing," she says.

▶By Ingrid Phaneuf   (09/98)

HEALTH

Field Coordinator
Clinical Research

■ What programme(s) I did:

B.A in Psychology, University of Montreal, Quebec
M.A. in Psychology, University of Montreal, Quebec

■ Average salary

$47 000

■ What are other possible routes to this position?

M.Sc. in Biology, Pure Sciences, or Health Sciences.

■ Skills and qualities you need for this job:

- need understanding of scientific method and bio-ethics
- need ability to co-ordinate large numbers of people
- need ability to meet deadlines and work well under pressure
- must have writing skills

"The Quality Cop"

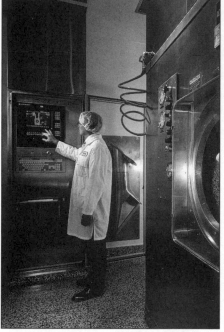

Jacques Soussy studied analytical chemistry to learn about laboratory analysis, only to find out it wasn't his calling. "I was never the type for lab work," he says. Jacques works as a Quality Assurance Technician at ICN Canada, a company which manufactures generic drugs, less costly "no name" alternatives to brand-name drugs. Luckily, Jacques can put his lab skills to use on his job without living in a lab. Roaming around his company, from lab to office to lab, it's his job to identify quality-control problems and make sure they get solved before ICN's drugs go on the market.

What I do

Quality assurance is the front line in the quality-control battle. Jacques' job is to catch problems in the early stages of production. "We are responsible for doing preliminary tests. I go to every department in our factory, gather samples and bring them back to the quality assurance lab for analysis, instructing staff on what needs to be done."

> **"We're a lot like cops, always keeping their eyes open to spot a suspicious character nearby."**

Jacques enjoys working in quality assurance — as opposed to quality control, done mostly in the laboratory. "In quality control, products are analysed by sophisticated equipment to find any contaminants. Staff don't get to move around much; all the work is in the lab".

Quality control is also the last resort. "Quality control does final testing of the product. If a problem is found at that stage, there's nothing the company can do but reject it and start over," explains Jacques.

Along with his two assistants, Jacques is responsible for inspecting nearly every aspect of the company's pill production. He verifies pill dosage, packaging and expiration dates (to see if the correct date has been marked). He even checks details such as the pills being in the right bottles, with the proper size caps. "Sometimes we make suggestions about equipment the company should buy or improvements in our facilities. Our factory is 70 years old, and doesn't have the very latest equipment, and sometimes we can trace a problem back to that."

Jacques compares his role to police work. "Often we find problems by pure chance, so we need to keep our eyes open. We don't just look at the floor when we're in the factory; we look everywhere. We're a lot like cops, always keeping their eyes open to spot a suspicious character nearby."

What skills do I need?

Jacques' training began with a Cegep-level analytical chemistry course, which provided an introduction to laboratory analysis. After that course, he worked in quality assurance as a summer job. "That's how I started out, and I found out that I enjoyed it much more than laboratory analysis. I prefer practical, hands-on work." For three years as a teenager he held summer jobs in quality control at food companies, and he knew he had found his calling.

Jacques holds a B.Sc. in Biology, but no specific university training for his current position at ICN. Upon graduation from university, he started working as a quality-control inspector in the pharmaceutical field. He felt at home right away in that particular role. "The key is to get as much experience in this field as possible."

Many universities offer a certificate in quality control, but Jacques only took a few quality-control courses and never completed a programme. It was "too theoretical" for his liking, he says. He learned most of what he knows on the job.

Jacques says that moral character is as important as skill in his job. "You must be honest; if there's a problem, you must report it. You can't hide it."

What is the work like?

Jacques and his assistants spend all their time on the go, looking for potential problems at this 120-employee, medium-sized plant. They have little time for coffee breaks during their intense, 39-hour workweek. "Our days are very full. We can count the number of quiet days in a year on the fingers of one hand." Overtime and weekend work add to his workload. Last year, Jacques put in nearly 300 overtime hours.

"If a problem slips by, it can have major consequences. We often catch serious problems, and that makes our work very motivating and satisfying."

There are also peak periods where Jacques is required to work more intensely. "We export some of our products, a few times a year. Those are the busiest times, and can mean coming in on weekends, or working until two in the morning."

Despite his workload, Jacques says he has no morale problems. He has to be on red alert all the time. "If a problem slips by, it can have major consequences. We often catch serious problems, and that makes our work very motivating and satisfying."

►By Wallie Seto and Sylvain Comeau (09/98)

HEALTH

Quality Assurance Technician
Quality Control

■ What programme(s) I did:

DEC in Analytical Chemistry, CEGEP de Vieux-Montréal, Quebec
DEC in Medical Laboratory Technology, CEGEP de Rosemont, Quebec
B.Sc. in Biology, University of Montreal, Quebec

■ Average salary

$34 239

■ What are other routes to this position?

Course or B.Sc. in Analytical Chemistry. Look for a programme that offers optional courses in quality control or quality assurance.

■ Skills and qualities you need for this job:

- must be able to locate and solve problems quickly
- must be alert and observant
- should enjoy teamwork

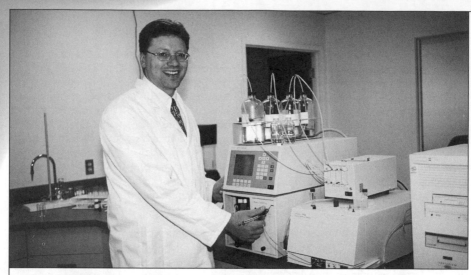

Photo : McMaster Photographers, Saskatoon

"The Smoother the Better"

Mark Hetherington believes that nature's products are still the best. He works for Fytochem Products Inc., a company which develops ingredients from plant extracts used by cosmetics and pharmaceutical companies to create products like skin creams. One of Fytokem's ingredients is derived from the willowherb, a plant native to north-western Canada that is used as an anti-irritant by U.S. cosmetics firm such as Aubrey Organics in their line of creams. "The cosmetic company puts the final product together. But it's our extract which actually soothes irritated skin," says Mark. As quality control manager at Fytokem, it is Mark's job to make sure nature actually does work best.

What I do

Mark joined Fytokem four years ago. He was Fytokem's first employee, and had to set up a quality control lab from scratch. As a product quality control manager, his mandate was to make sure Fytokem would produce exactly the same ingredient from one year to the next, and that the ingredient would not be altered or contaminated in the lab before shipment to customers.

Mark's job involves some skills traditionally reserved for researchers. The first thing he must do is to figure out exactly what substance in each extract has a therapeutic effect (such as soothing irritated skin). "An extract will contain a certain collection of chemicals. You need to determine what chemicals are responsible for what effects, and the levels at which those chemicals are present in extracts, before you can manufacture the product."

> **"Our clients have to feel confident that a certain product will always perform the same way."**

The next thing Mark must do is make sure the product doesn't change, either during the time it is being processed, or from one year to the next. "Our clients have to feel confident that a certain product will always perform the same way." He does this by taking and testing samples from batches of extracts.

Mark's research and development skills sometimes find other uses besides quality control at Fytokem. "There can be thousands of chemicals in one plant extract

Sometimes I'm asked to look a little bit further into the extract, to see what else is in there. That might lead to other uses for the product."

What skills
do I need?

Mark has a Master's degree in Analytical Chemistry, including quality analysis and quality control training. He was aiming for a job as an analytical chemist, which means analysing samples to see what chemicals are present, and in what quantity. "That skill is perfectly suited for quality analysis and quality control," he says.

As quality control manager, Mark needs initiative and a broad view of his projects. "In order to set up my own lab, I had to find out what work we would be doing, what analysis we would need, and what would be the best instrumentation to get the job done. Then I had to look at our budget and decide what we could afford."

Mark's work environment is a bit of a contradiction: noisy, but at the same time intellectual and focused.

Mark says that certain interpersonal skills are also essential to his job. "A manager must act as a coach. My management style is that I believe in encouraging the people I work with, and I keep up to date on their progress and encourage them while instructing them."

What is
the work like?

There is no such thing as a typical workday for Mark, although some routine duties have to be repeated everyday. "I start the day by making sure that all my instrumentation is functioning properly," he says. "Then I usually have some samples to analyse. Sometimes that can be routine analysis in which our instruments are set up to look for one specific chemical."

Mark's work environment is a bit of a contradiction: noisy, but at the same time intellectual and focused. "There are always instruments running, which means a constant background noise. But the environment is an academic one; there's a lot of work being done at a fast pace, but in a controlled manner."

He says that job pressure varies, depending on the company's deadlines. "Now we're in the early stages of our development as a company. Currently, I have no problem keeping up with the work, but later, when the large orders start flying out the door, then the job will become pressure-packed."

"The pressure comes not only from deadlines, but also from the fact that quality control people are the first to get blamed if something goes wrong. You're going to be the first person that people come back to if the product is not what they say it is."

▶By Wallie Seto and Sylvain Comeau (09/98)

HEALTH

Quality Control Manager
Quality Control

■ What programme(s) I did:

B.Sc. in Chemistry, U. of Saskatchewan, Saskatchewan
M.Sc. in Analytical Chemistry, University of Saskatchewan, Saskatchewan

■ Average salary

$66 964

■ What are other possible routes to this position?

B.Sc. in either Biology, Biochemistry or Microbiology is a minimum requirement. A graduate degree (Master's or Ph.D.) in these fields is even better. Courses are offered by professional associations like the Canadian Institute of Chemistry.

■ Skills and qualities you need for this job:

- must be meticulous and detail-oriented
- need strong organisation skills
- computer literacy is essential
- should be an independent, creative thinker

Photo : PPM, Montreal

"The Research Clinic Coach"

Patrick Colin is interested in stomach aches, but even more interested in what makes them go away. He is director of clinical research at Axcan Pharma, a company of 120 employees dedicated to the research, development, production and marketing of products for use in gastroenterology. Four-fifths of the drugs Axcan develops are used for diagnosing and treating problems of the esophagus, stomach, small and large intestines, gallbladder, liver or pancreas. "I always thought that in medicine, what treats and cures people is, above all, the drugs," says Patrick.

What I do

As director of clinical research, Patrick does not actually work on cures for these problems. Patrick is not a research scientist, he's a manager. He is in charge of implementing Axcan's clinical research programmes, a task which involves finding the right doctors to carry out tests on humans and making sure they follow the exact instructions for testing.

Axcan works both on its own drugs and new indications, or new uses for existing drugs, like aspirin for example, which was first used to relieve pain but was later discovered to be effective in reducing the risk of heart attacks. Patrick spends much of his day meeting with researchers and the company's executives to decide what projects to pursue. Axcan does not do research and development from scratch; the bulk of its efforts, and Patrick's, go into testing products on humans to assess their effectiveness.

When Patrick started working for Axcan in 1994, part of his job was putting together its research department and programmes. Now he makes sure the projects Axcan undertakes run smoothly. In a way you could compare him to an athletic coach. After the company has decided what type of drug it wants to develop, Patrick must put together the best possible team for the job. Then he decides what rules he wants them to follow, creating what is known as a research protocol. This stipulates how many subjects will be tested, their sex and age-group, and what specific treatment they will be given.

"I would say that half of my day is made up of meetings and discussions about the course of research programmes, studies, protocols and picking investigators to conduct our studies. The other half is spent preparing documents and protocols," he says.

What skills
do I need?

"I have always been interested in the pharmaceutical industry and in developing new drugs," says Patrick. "The combination of medical, chemical and other knowledge attracted me." This interest eventually led him to pharmaceutical studies. He graduated with a B.Sc., M.Sc. and Ph.D. in Pharmacy from the University of Montreal.

Patrick says that work in the pharmaceutical or biotechnology industry calls for a high educational level. "It's important to have basic biomedical training as well as research experience. So you need at least a Master's or a Ph.D."

Patrick's travels take him all over North America.

Patrick says success in management calls for versatility. "Product development is not a specialised activity. It requires knowledge in pharmacology, chemistry, medicine, etc. It's a very complex endeavour." Like the hockey coach who needs to know about defence, attack and goal-keeping, Patrick has to be able to talk to a doctor about a sophisticated research process while keeping the commercial aspect of the end product in mind.

But training is not everything, according to Patrick, who feels that an open mind and desire to learn are also essential. "You need scientific curiosity because we're always looking for new ideas," he says. "You also have to be comfortable with the medical community, which means being able to speak the same language as the doctors with whom you work."

What is
the work like?

Patrick generally works from 9 to 6, in an office environment where he spends most of his time in meetings and on the phone. However, he says 40% of his overall time is actually spent on the road. "I have to meet with the doctors who work on our clinical studies regularly to assess progress. I also have to attend scientific conferences and symposiums." Patrick's travels take him all over North America.

His favourite part of the job is following a product from the time it's just an idea to its launch on the market. "When you work in a small company, as opposed to a multinational, you often have the chance to be exposed to all the facets of product development. We're involved from the beginning of clinical research to commercialisation. It's a process that can take years."

▶By Christine Daviault   (09/98)

ᴗHEALTH

Senior Clinical Executive
Clinical Research

■ What programme(s) I did:

B.Sc. in Pharmacy, University of Montreal, Quebec
M.Sc. in Pharmacy, University of Montreal, Quebec
Ph.D. in Pharmacy, University of Montreal, Quebec

■ Average salary
$137 631

■ What are other routes to this position?

A background in medicine, chemistry, or biochemistry.

■ Skills and qualities you need for this job:

- need to be versatile
- need to be bilingual
- need to be a leader, enjoy organising
- scientific curiosity is an assett

77

"The Fish Doctor"

Catherine Bone never wanted a desk job. She's happy every morning putting on heavy rubber boots to go to work, where she keeps 30 000 salmon healthy so that her company, Aqua Health, can test experimental vaccines on them.

Photo : David Macneil Photographer, Charlottetown

What I do

Catherine works in a giant two-room aquarium filled with circular salmon tanks that let water flow in a soft current. She spends most of her time cleaning the tanks, feeding the salmon and giving them their medicine!

Catherine's wetlab is the final and crucial step in Aqua Health's project of creating fish vaccines that protect farmed salmon from disease. The first step is creating the vaccine, which Catherine's colleagues do by collecting bacteria from infected fish and growing it in huge fermentation tanks. They kill the bacteria, mix it with either water or oil and place it in a large plastic bag that looks like a blood bag. Then they give it to Catherine to test on the fish.

> **In the challenge room Catherine cleans and disinfects tanks for two groups of fish — a control group that has not been vaccinated and a group of vaccinated salmon.**

The first thing Catherine does is test the vaccine on healthy fish. In the larger "safety" room of the aquarium which holds disease-free salmon, Catherine selects anywhere from 400 to 1400 healthy salmon and either injects them with the vaccine or places the vaccine in their water to be absorbed through their gills. Then she leaves the fish to fight the bacteria. If they do so without getting sick or dying, the vaccine is considered safe. Then the vaccine is ready to be tested on diseased fish in the "challenge" room to see whether it actually wards off disease.

In the challenge room Catherine cleans and disinfects tanks for two groups of fish — a control group that has not been vaccinated and a group of vaccinated salmon. She counts out and transfers a specified number of healthy fish to the tanks and adds the disease bacteria to their water.

> **She used to wish that she hadn't bothered with university at all, but her opinion has changed over the last year.**

Then Catherine watches to see how many fish die. As they die, she puts them into a plastic bag and marks the bag to identify whether it was in the control group or the vaccinated group. Later, she scrapes the fish kidneys onto a small glass plate covered in chemicals that show what killed the fish. "In the ideal case," she says, all the control fish which were infected with the bug but never vaccinated die, and all the vaccinated fish don't die." That proves a vaccine works.

What skills
do I need?

Although Catherine has a university degree in marine biology, she completed a 48-week college course to become an aqua-cultural technician before she found a job in her field. She used to wish that she hadn't bothered with university at all, but her opinion has changed over the last year. "Now that I've been here for a while I think the university courses have really helped me. I was expecting to work in a hatchery when I finished my college course, but because I had university training I was able to get this type of a job that is more research-oriented. This is a very mature environment—I don't think I could have come here as an 18-year-old."

Catherine spent 13 weeks of her college course working as an unpaid trainee in the industry. Then AquaHealth asked her instructor to recommend someone for a 16-week temporary placement. Catherine was interviewed on a Friday and offered the job the following Monday. Just as her temporary posting was ending, someone else at the company went on maternity leave so she stayed. AquaHealth liked her so much that they found her a full time job.

What is
the work like?

Catherine works from 8 a.m. until 5 p.m. with an hour for lunch. She spends much of her day alone feeding the salmon, removing the ones that die and cleaning the tanks. The job usually takes up most of the morning.

Catherine isn't sure where her present work will lead. "In our company, the wetlab is the place you start."

She vaccinates fish right after lunch. On days when there are no vaccinations to be done, she sets up challenges, accepts deliveries from hatcheries or learns new skills from other departments, like doing environmental testing in the building to see if there is bacteria on the premises. She also does maintenance, making sure her equipment is functioning properly.

Catherine isn't sure where her present work will lead. "In our company, the wetlab is the place you start," she says. "I don't really know how far I can move up, but I think that the things I'm learning here are going to be invaluable for the rest of my life. They're willing to train me to do anything."

►By Tracey Arial   (09/98)

AQUACULTURE

Animal Care
Manufacturing/ Field Work

■ What programme(s) I did:

B.Sc. in Marine Biology, University of New Brunswick, New Brunswick
Aquacultural Technician Programme, New Brunswick Community College, New Brunswick

■ Average salary

$30 000

■ What are other routes to this position?

A B.Sc. in Biology, veterinary college courses or other aquaculture technician courses.

■ Skills and qualities you need for this job:

- need background in applied science
- must be able to work independently
- need to be organised and methodical
- should enjoy working hands-on with animals

Photo : PPM, Montreal

"The Quality Engineer"

Merck Frosst, Canada's leading pharmaceutical company, is recognised as an industry leader in the research and development of new medicines for asthma, heart disease, HIV/Aids and osteoporosis, to name a few. Merck Frosst is a related company of Merck & Co. Inc., a multinational pharmaceutical company with offices and plants world-wide. As an engineering manager, part of **Bernard Boisvert's** job is to make sure Merck Frosst keeps up its world-wide reputation for quality medication. "Our customers expect our products to be consistent and of high quality. They don't want surprises. When they take medicine for an illness, they expect it to work."

What I do

Bernard works as a manager in the engineering department at Merck Frosst's facility in the Montreal suburb of Kirkland. The buildings, including the offices, laboratories and manufacturing plant, take up more than 700 000 square feet. The company markets tablets such as Singulair for asthmatics, Vasotec for high blood pressure

and Zocor for people with high cholesterol levels.

Bernard works with three other engineering managers and supervises more than 60 technicians, mechanics and tradespersons. His job is to make sure that the facility is well maintained and that the equipment is performing properly. Bernard doesn't fix broken machines; his job is to find the best mechanics and technicians for the job and to make sure it gets done.

Trouble shooting — anticipating and reacting to breakdowns and malfunctions — is one of Bernard's most important tasks. He is responsible for making sure all equipment is tested, evaluated and maintained according to industry standards and government regulations. It's a crucial task, he says, both for the company and for consumers of its products. For instance, when all tablets of a particular medication are the same, it means the patient gets a consistent dose to improve his or her health.

What skills do I need?

A university degree in engineering is a prerequisite for Bernard's job. Bernard says his own university education provided him with a technical background and an in-depth knowledge of how sophisticated equipment works. But his real engineering education began much earlier than university, he says. "I took physics and chemistry courses in high school. But it all started with doing well in math, which is the basis of all sciences."

In addition to technical knowledge, Bernard says finance and accounting skills are important in order to be able to set annual budgets and keep track of expenses on a monthly basis. Bernard is also fluent in French and English — essential in his work environment in Quebec — but he wishes he knew more languages! "It's good to know as many languages as possible. A multinational company like ours has offices all over the world."

Bernard says he can't overemphasise the importance of being able to work in teams. "You have to be willing and able to help others so they'll help you when you need it." Managing people is also important, he says. There are 100 employees and managers who work in the engineering department at Montreal's MerckFrosst plant! "Part of our job is dealing with people's needs and problems. We provide a service and we're there to make sure that the whole facility is working smoothly. That not only includes the manufacturing equipment but the ventilation and the building structure as well."

What is
the work like?

Being a manager means having more responsibilities than other employees. This is part of the reason Bernard works 40 to 50 hours per week. He has a regular Monday to Friday week, but goes in on weekends for emergencies.

He starts work at 7:30 a.m. by reading his e-mail and replying to phone messages to find out what happened overnight. The rest of Bernard's day is all improvisation. His responsibilities include meeting with other managers to keep up to date on the activities of the departments, and co-ordinating tests, calibrations and repairs of production equipment.

Bernard takes home the work he can't get done during the regular working day. He spends two or three evenings a week reading work-related documents such as trade magazines and newsletters. He also carries home a laptop computer to write monthly reports.

"The good part of my job is that there's very little routine. I especially like it when something out of the ordinary happens. A difficult problem will come up, we'll work on it and find a solution for it. I find that challenge very satisfying."

▶By Wallie Seto and Sylvain Comeau (09/98)

HEALTH

Biotech Engineer
Manufacturing/Field Work

■ What programme(s) I did:

B.Sc. in Physical Engineering, University of Montreal - École Polytechnique, Quebec

■ Average salary

$45 000

■ What are other possible routes to this position?

Undergraduate degrees in civil, electrical or mechanical engineering. Some business training is helpful.

■ Skills and qualities you need for this job:

- knowledge of how equipment and machinery works
- must be able to set and manage budgets
- should be flexible, able to solve problems on short notice

81

"The Scientific Talent Scout"

Photo : Patrick Villeneuve, Montreal

A good idea and hard work aren't enough to get a biotech company going. Start-up companies usually need money too. In Montreal, many companies turn to Société Innovatech du Grand Montréal (Innovatech Montreal), a venture capital fund providing start-up cash to new high-technology companies in exchange for part-ownership. However, to perform its role, Innovatech needs to assess which companies will pay off. That's **Sylvie Masson's** job. As business development analyst, she judges whether biotech companies' science is strong enough to merit investment funds.

What I do

Sylvie is a scientific analyst, one of three people examining business plans from the biotechnology sector. "The scientific project is the first thing we analyse, because it will be the focus of the company." she says. "It has to be long-lasting. A company looking for new antibiotics could be a good investment," says Sylvie, to provide a simple example of her job. "Society always needs more antibiotics because bacteria build up resistance to them."

After determining that a biotechnology project has a good long-term focus, Sylvie has to make sure that the scientists involved have the research, credibility, patience and methods to actually achieve their goal. She sometimes hires a specialist to help her scrutinise all the details.

As Sylvie analyses the science, a financial analyst makes sure that the numbers in the business plan add up, and a director examines the project's business feasability. Their work usually takes about three months. Then they present projects they like to their own board for approval. Innovatech has already funded 35 new companies in the biotechnology sector this way, and Sylvie is currently examining another 20.

She says a business-science combination is a rare, desirable commodity in the job market.

Sylvie's team continues in-depth analysis for the first six months of any new company start-up. Then they follow the company's progress by sitting on its board (Sylvie currently sits on four). After five or six years, a new biotech company is usually ready to merge with a larger company or go public (meaning it then raises money by selling shares on the stock market). Then Innovatech's role ends. It sells its shares in the company and uses the money to help another venture.

What skills do I need?

Sylvie has a B.Sc. and a M.Sc. in Biology from Laval University in Quebec City. After that, she completed four years of a Ph.D. at University of Montreal and most of a Master's in Business Administration (MBA) programme. She says such a business-science combination is a rare, desirable commodity in the job market. "A lot of venture capital funds and banks are looking for people with both degrees."

After her Ph.D. studies, Sylvie spent five or six years cloning and sequencing genes in a genetic engineering research lab. She realised then that lab work was not for her. "I wanted to work more with people than with test-tubes." Sylvie decided to start an MBA degree at the École des hautes études commerciales, the business school affiliated with U of M. About half way through her degree, she heard about the job at Innovatech Montréal. It seemed the perfect way to leave the lab while broadening her scientific knowledge. "Innovatech Montréal was what I was looking for when I started my MBA," says Sylvie.

Sylvie says her type of work requires friendliness and good listening skills. She says she relies on intuition to size people up. "I have to feel that the person I see will be someone with whom I can work," she says.

As a new biotechnology company's part-owner's representative, Sylvie will work with each of her clients for at least five years.

What is the work like?

Sylvie is one of 18 employees at a very team-oriented venture capital firm. Everyone spends a lot of time discussing their files with other employees. Sylvie also spends half the week outside the office, meeting clients and other investors or attending board meetings.

Sylvie feels she has the world's best job.

Sylvie normally arrives at 8 or 8:30 in the morning and leaves around 6 p.m., but often works late. She is particularly busy when a potential client has been approved and must go before Innovatech's board for funding.

Sylvie shares an office with a view of Montreal's Mount Royal. She spends most of her time on the phone, on the Internet or meeting with colleagues. She feels she has the world's best job. "I look through colourful and interesting scientific projects. I work with very skilled scientists. I learn about different subjects all the time. Every day brings a new project and a new subject."

►By Tracey Arial   (09/98)

Business Development Analyst
Sales and Marketing

■ What programme(s) I did:

B.Sc. in Biology, Laval University, Quebec
M.Sc. in Biology, Laval University, Quebec
Science Administration Diploma from the École des hautes études commerciales, Quebec

■ Average salary

$73 446

■ What are other routes to this position?

Any strong science background combined with business background.

■ Skills and qualities you need for this job:

- need to be curious
- must have critical thinking skills
- need lab experience
- need business skills

Photo : Lyle Stafford, Vancouver

"Selling Solutions Abroad"

After almost a decade working for prestigious computer companies, and a four-year stint at an aircraft manufacturer in Tokyo, **Deborah Bird** made a dramatic career change. She joined StemCell Technologies Inc., a small company that makes specialised products for biotech researchers. As business development manager, her job is to find distributors outside North America for StemCell's products. "I get a lot of gratification from feeling like I'm contributing to some good for other people rather than just earning big bucks," she says.

What I do

StemCell creates over 150 products vital to cancer research, including a gel-like substance that enables blood cells to grow in a laboratory, a horseshoe-shaped magnetic device that allows scientists to separate particular types of cells from blood and bone marrow, and specialised computer software that enables researchers to obtain statistics about people who have had bone marrow transplants.

The people who actually use StemCell's products are doctors and researchers involved in projects such as bone marrow transplants and leukemia and HIV research. Researchers are StemCell's actual clients, but the company doesn't deal with those who live outside North America directly. Instead, StemCell relies on people or companies located in specific regions all over the world to actually sell to researchers. To find distributors, Deborah spends a lot of time on the phone talking to current StemCell clients, to researchers, and even to schools to see if they know of potential distributors.

Deborah is in charge of knowing all the ins and outs of importing and exporting. "Whenever we run into problems trying to get the product into another country, I sort through whatever paperwork is necessary and put procedures in place," she says. When there was a scare about a disease that affects cows ("blue tongue", not "mad cow" disease), Deborah had some challenging work to do, because many of StemCell's products contain cells from cows.

Deborah also handles any large international projects in which StemCell is involved. When StemCell Technologies recently opened their own office in France, for example, it was Deborah who arranged to hire the employees, rent office space, and set up the whole operation.

What skills
do I need?

Deborah is StemCell's first business development manager. "I'm not actually sure what Business Development Managers are supposed to do!" she says. "This job developed around skills and experience I already had."

Deborah has a computer science diploma from Mohawk College in Hamilton, Ontario. Her programme allowed her to complete three work terms at Honeywell. After graduating, she moved to IBM Canada, where she stayed for seven years. These jobs gave Deborah the solid understanding of corporate culture essential for her current job while providing her with handy computer skills. The first thing she did at StemCell, for example, was replace an outdated customer database system. She also set up a network between the computers of the administrative office in downtown Vancouver and the laboratory outside the city.

Deborah also picked up a strong understanding of international corporate culture by running an information systems office that aircraft manufacturer McDonnell Douglas owned in Tokyo. She spent four years learning about Asia and its business practices by selling software to large international corporations like Toshiba and Fujitsu. She also picked up experience dealing with corporate lawyers. She is presently putting that exper-

tise to good use drawing up a standard agreement for StemCell's distributors.

Deborah feels that working abroad gave her another invaluable skill: understanding cultural differences and learning to adapt to them, a basic requirement for her work at StemCell.

What is
the work like?

About once a year, Deborah plans a trip overseas to meet with some of her clients face-to-face. However, most of her communication with them is via fax, email or phone. She spends most days at her desk, in her office in Vancouver, speaking to people in Europe, Asia, Australia and South America.

Deborah usually gets to the office at 8:00 a.m. so she can still reach the Europeans at the end of their day, (European time is at least 8 hours ahead of Vancouver time). Then she checks her email and handles any distributor-related concerns.

After this morning routine, she checks her calendar for the day's appointments, and begins preparing the information she needs for meetings and discussions with potential clients.

Deborah spends the last part of her day, from about 4 until 5:30 p.m., catching up with her Asian clients. She also has a computer at home and provides all the distributors with her home number so that they can reach her in any emergency.

▶By Tracey Arial   (09/98)

HEALTH

Business Development Manager
Sales and Marketing

■ **What programme(s) I did:**

Diploma in Computer Programming from Mohawk College, Hamilton, Ontario

■ **Average salary**

$92,060

■ **What are other routes to this position?**

The qualifications for the profession are still being defined. Familiarity with business practices and some knowledge of science are essential.

■ **Skills and qualities you need for the job:**

- need skills in developing relationships
- need general understanding of intellectual property
- should have experience in other cultures
- must have good negotiation skills

"The Decontaminator

Jason Chiasson rarely sees the inside of an office; he's too busy in the field, where the action is. As field technician for Geobac Technology Group, a company that specialises in decontaminating soil and groundwater, Jason's job is supervising the team that cleans up environmental messes such as oil and gas spills.

What I do

Geobac specialises in bioremediation, which means making contaminated land usable again. Most of the company's clients are businesses like gas stations or oil refineries. If a company has spilled or leaked toxic substances into the ground and the ground water, they call on Geobac to get rid of the oil and stop the leak.

> **"I'm usually trying to do two or three jobs at the same time; I do everything from the drilling, to making a record of the samples we take, to shipping them off to the lab."**

The company cleans up the spill with special bacteria that feed on petroleum. Jason starts by determining how much oil leaked, if it hit the water table, and how much cleanup is required. Then he drills deep monitoring wells, so he can collect ground water samples to test how much contamination has taken place and where.

He also measures air quality using a handheld gauge, and submits all his findings to his boss. Then he adds the bacteria to the soil.

Sometimes Jason works alone, and sometimes he supervises a team of up to a dozen workers. But supervision work still means getting his hands dirty. "I'm usually trying to do two or three jobs at the same time; I do everything from the drilling, to making a record of the samples we take, to shipping them off to the lab," he explains.

What skills do I need?

Jason joined Geomac three years ago. He took the job soon after graduating from the Environmental Technology programme at New Brunswick Community College. While he was doing this programme, Jason took every science course that would fit into his

86

schedule. These included an analytical chemistry course, where he learned how to do water quality and air quality tests to help pinpoint the source of a leak. Through hydrogeology, he learned how to dig and maintain monitoring wells. And microbiology courses taught him how to examine soil for damage.

> **"You have to be calm and collected; you can't let things get to you. You have to be able to adjust quickly to new situations, because this kind of job is very spontaneous."**

"I learned how to look for biological indicators. For example, certain odours or vegetation growth can mean that there is contamination present."

Writing and math skills are also indispensable. "I write a lot of reports and have to get the wording just right, for legal reasons," he says. "Lawsuits are common in the business." Jason says math skills are necessary to calculate the dimensions of the materials he needs to order. His line of work also requires several personal qualities. "You have to be calm and collected; you can't let things get to you. You have to be able to adjust quickly to new situations, because this kind of job is very spontaneous." You also have to stay on your toes, and roll with the punches, he says. "You can't be too excitable, because things happen. If you don't have certain materials, for example, you deal with it. And it helps if you enjoy the great outdoors."

What is the work like?

Jason enjoys his job, despite often working long hours on many projects. He admits that juggling tasks during a project is tough and challenging.

"Sometimes I'm drilling, and I'm trying to keep control of the machine, and at the same time I'm trying to log my samples. I get my hands dirty, and I'm trying to keep my papers clean...it's very frustrating."

Being a field technician also means living out of a suitcase a lot of the time. "You have to be ready to travel a lot. This job is really a life on the road, so you have to like being on the move and away from home." Jason also has to be ready to drop everything and rush out on a job at a moment's notice. "I've actually had a 15-minute notice that I had to work on a property three hours away. I had to jump in my vehicle and go right away. So sometimes it gets pretty stressful."

For Jason, job satisfaction comes from his contribution to environmental protection. "I've always been interested in ecological concerns. Everyone talks about the environment, but not everyone does something about it. I'm lucky, because I'm in a position to make a difference."

►By Wallie Seto and Sylvain Comeau (09/98)

ENVIRONMENT

Field Technician
Manufacturing/ Field Work

■ What programme(s) I did:

Diploma in Environmental Technology,
New Brunswick Community College, New Brunswick

■ Average salary

$47 000

■ What are other routes to this position?

B.Sc. in Biology, Chemistry or other basic science programme.
B.Sc. in Ecotoxicology or other science-oriented environmental programme.

■ Skills and qualities you need for this job:

- must be well organised
- must be able to improvise, think on your feet
- need writing and math skills
- should enjoy travelling

"Risks and Rewards"

Today, anyone can own a piece of the biotechnology future by buying biotech shares on the stock market. But it is often difficult to assess which companies have the most promising technology, and which might fail. That is where **Jean-Luc Berger** comes in. Jean-Luc is a financial analyst specialising in biotecholocy. He uses his scientific and financial knowledge to serve the growing need for information about the dynamic but risky biotechnology industry.

Photo : Daniels & Gilonna Photography, Toronto

What I do

Credifinance Securities Ltd. is a Toronto-based brokerage firm which offers financial services such as research on companies. It also helps various companies find partners with which they can merge, or licensing and sales partners.

Jean-Luc's clients are mutual fund companies, insurance companies, and other big financial institutions interested in investing in biotech. They hire him to write research reports on biotech companies — usually small ones in the early technological development stages. "I investigate whether or not a particular company has a promising future, and whether it would be a good idea to invest in that company."

To assess a company and its research projects, Jean-Luc must have an excellent understanding of the specific research they are doing - whether it involves developing a new HIV treatment or a new cancer remedy.

The reports are based on a lot of factors: the strength of the company's technology, the market for their product, the existing competition and whether or not they have partnerships with other companies. He also looks at management competence, whether or not the company has patented its technology, the strength and clarity of its business plan and how far a company's research has come.

To assess a company and its research projects, Jean-Luc must have an excellent understanding of the specific research they are doing - whether it involves developing a new HIV treatment or a new cancer remedy. Before writing a report, he spends several weeks doing his own research. He does Internet searches, combs through newspapers and research journals, and phones up experts for information on the company and the industry. He then takes a few weeks to write up his reports, which are often 20 or 30 pages long.

Jean-Luc is also expected to prepare brief updates for his clients on recent stock market events, to explain why stock prices are rising, falling or not changing.

What skills do I need?

Jean-Luc has a Ph.D. in Food Science and Technology from Laval University in Quebec City. He decided to become a financial analyst, he says, to "fulfil a dream of working on Bay Street," the heart of Toronto's financial district. Training in both business and science is essential for his job. "Most financial analysts can read and assess a company's financial statements, but they usually don't know what the company's science is worth. The biotechnology industry needs financial analysts who can evaluate the science as well."

Today, he notes, most financial analysts in biotech combine a pharmaceutical degree or an M.Sc. or Ph.D. in another scientific discipline with training in business and administration.

For his job, Jean-Luc also needs good communications skills: he has to be able to explain difficult concepts to people who don't necessarily have a scientific background.

What is the work like?

"Twelve hours on the job," Jean-Luc answers with a laugh, when asked to describe a typical workday. "The stock market closes at four every day, but that doesn't make it a 9-to-5 job. If anything unusual happens in biotechnology, I have to write a brief on it for my clients the next morning. For example, if a company fails in a trial of its new drug, I have to write about it fast, before the markets open in the morning." Jean-Luc's day starts at 7:30 in the morning. The first thing he does when he gets to the office is catch up on the latest news about the companies he is researching.

The best part of the job is working close to an industry which is developing the technology of tomorrow.

"This work is very hard, very tiring. I've known several people in this business who left to do something else after only three or four months. They were very smart, brilliant people with Ph.D.s and M.B.A.s, but they couldn't handle the pressure." Enjoying the work, and being able to keep up morale during long hours is a requirement for success in the field.

The best part of the job, Jean-Luc says, is working close to an industry which is developing the technology of tomorrow. "The most satisfying thing is working on cutting edge technology, and with new medications on the front lines in the battle against disease. I learn about a whole variety of research areas, and that's exciting."

▶By Wallie Seto and Sylvain Comeau (09/98)

GETTING PRODUCTS OUT THERE

HEALTH

Financial Analyst
Sales and Marketing

■ What programme(s) I did:

B.Sc. in Microbiology, University of Montreal, Quebec
M.Sc. in Microbiology and Immunology, University of Montreal, Quebec
Ph.D. in Food Science and Technology, Laval University, Quebec
Post-Doctoral Fellowship, McGill University, Quebec

■ Average salary

$54 123

■ What are other routes to this position?

To become a financial analyst, students need a business degree, such as an M.B.A. or a C.F.A. (Chartered Financial Analyst) designation. To work as a financial analyst in biotech, a combined science degree and business degree is required.

■ Skills and qualities you need for this job:

- need strong analytical skills
- must have a general knowledge of the stock market
- need a good knowledge of science
- must be able to explain complex ideas

89

"Backup Bill"

Photo : Daniels & Gilonna Photography, Toronto

A biotech company starts off as an idea. A person or a group of researchers believe they can create a better treatment for cancer, for example. They found their company, convince people to invest money in the project, hire employees and start the process of making that idea a product which can be sold.

During this process, a company may encounter difficulties or problems. Their research programme may not produce results as fast as they had planned. They may need more investments in the company but don't know where to turn for the capital. In situations like this, companies can find help and advice in the person of **Bill Dobson**, an industrial technology adviser.

What I do

Bill works for the Industrial Research Assistance Programme (IRAP) which is sponsored by the National Research Council of Canada. IRAP is made of up 250 Industrial Technology Advisers based across the country who work with small and medium-sized businesses (under 500 employees) focused on areas like biotechnology.

To give good advice, Bill must first understand as completely as possible what a company is trying to accomplish.

Advisers help companies figure out their technical needs (deciding how many new employees to hire and in what areas) as well as helping them to find financial assistance (government investment programmes or private investments). Advisers also help companies find research partners for collaborative projects.

Bill insists on having an office on the University of Toronto's main campus in order to be close to scientists and researchers.

"We work very closely with the company, often for two or three months at a time," Bill explains. Recently a biotech company working on cancer drugs asked for help. Bill met with them and realised that they needed to rethink their research programme. He pointed out ways they could more easily produce some of the chemicals needed for the drugs. As a result, the company will be able to make the drugs more quickly. Bill also helped them to find three other companies interested in creating a research partnership to create new products.

What skills do I need?

"You have to be very patient and you have to know the right questions to ask and when to ask them," Bill says. To give good advice, Bill must first understand as completely as possible what a company is trying to accomplish. Getting that clear picture requires listening skills, tact and a deep knowledge of the biotech industry.

To keep up to date on biotech issues, "I try to spend at least two days a month in a lab talking with a researcher or meeting with a university professor to talk about what is happening in the industry," Bill says. He also insists on having an office on the University of Toronto's main campus in order to be close to scientists and researchers. (The IRAP regional office is based in a suburb of Toronto.)

"You start when you have to start and you finish when the work is done." "It's definitely not a nine-to-five job."

Bill was always attracted to a career in science. "My dad was a microbiologist and I grew up with microscopes at home." Bill completed a Bachelor's degree in biology and a Ph.D. in microbiology and biochemistry at the University of Windsor. He spent almost 15 years working for private companies in several different areas of biotechnology: research, manufacturing, quality assurance and regulatory affairs (working with the government to get drugs approved). He joined IRAP in 1993. "My industry knowledge in biotech was very important to getting this job."

What is the work like?

Bill's office is located in a building on the University of Toronto campus. He spends about 25 per cent of his time at the office, mostly talking on the telephone to companies or other advisers or writing reports about his work. He works alone. "It's just me at the office," he says. "I do my own typing and faxing."

About 75 per cent of Bill's time is spent meeting with companies. He travels frequently within Ontario and regularly across Canada. With his expertise in biotechnology, Bill is often asked to help advisers working with companies outside Ontario. When he's meeting with companies, Bill says, it's not unusual for him to work 12 to 14 hours a day. "You start when you have to start and you finish when the work is done," he says. "It's definitely not a nine-to-five job."

"Biotechnology changes so quickly. You have to stay focused so you don't get left in its wake."

Bill says the challenge of his job is the one facing the biotechnology field as a whole: to keep up with the rapid changes and find ways to make biotechnology benefit people. "Biotechnology changes so quickly. You have to stay focused so you don't get left in its wake," he says.

▶By Liz Warwick   (09/98)

Industrial Adviser
Sales and Marketing

■ What programme(s) I did:

B.Sc. in Biology, University of Windsor, Ontario
Ph.D. in Microbiology and Biochemistry, University of Windsor, Ontario

■ Average salary

$60 000

■ What are other routes to this position?

A Bachelor's and probably Master's degree in science or engineering field. All ITA's have at least five years' minimum experience in industry. A Ph.D. is not required.

■ Skill and qualities you need for this job:

- must be patient, enjoy helping people
- must have excellent listening skills
- should have broad and up-to-date knowledge of biotech industry
- must be tenacious, thorough

"Putting Money Where it Matters"

Photo : Daniels & Gilonna Photography, Toronto

The Cangene Corporation, a biopharmaceutical company which develops and markets brand-name and generic drugs, is a publicly-traded company. Anyone can buy shares in it — providing Cangene with the funds it needs to develop new drugs — and then receive a percentage of the company's profits in return. However, before buying shares, investors understandably want to know a little more about what Cangene is, and what it is doing with their money. That's where **Jean Compton** comes in.

What I do

Jean Compton takes care of investor relations at Cangene. It's her responsibility to make sure potential investors hear about the company, that investors get answers to their questions and that Cangene fulfils its legal responsibilities as a publicly-traded company.

Keeping financial analysts up to date on developments at Cangene is essential; their approval is a key factor in attracting potential investors.

Jean's work involves communicating with individual or institutional investors on a one-on-one basis or through documents she provides to the public. She is responsible for writing annual reports. These are magazine-size documents describing Cangene's work, outlining progress or changes in its projects during the preceding year and providing a full update on Cangene's finances. She also writes quarterly reports, smaller versions of the above, made available to investors and financial analysts four times per year on specific dates set forth by the government.

Jean must also keep an up-to-date list of investors and their addresses in order to make sure they get the information they require. These reports must also be filed to securities commissions and to stock exchanges, and must be made available to anyone who requests them. They are even posted on the company's web site. All this means Jean handles a lot of paperwork, and juggles a lot of deadlines.

Jean also has to speak to investors one-on-one, and answer questions from potential investors and stockbrokers (the people who buy stocks for investors). She meets and speaks regularly with financial analysts who publish their own reports on how they think a company is doing. The analysts' reports help their own clients decide where to invest their money. Keeping financial analysts up to date on developments at Cangene is essential; their approval is a key factor in attracting potential investors.

Jean also writes press releases to attract new investors through the media, makes presentations to groups of investors and helps the president and CEO prepare investor presentations. "The information you put out is the backbone of a publicly-owned company," says Jean. "That's what gives you value in the eyes of shareholders. If no one knows what's going on in your company, no one will buy shares."

What skills
do I need?

Jean has a B.Sc. in Genetics from the University of Guelph and studied marketing at Ryerson, in Toronto. But her training came mostly on the job. She's been at Cangene for 14 years. She started out as a research technician, then became a lab manager and purchasing manager. When the company went public in Oct. 1991, Cangene needed someone to answer stock holders' questions. Because of her knowledge and experience at Cangene, Jean was the firm's first choice.

Since she started dealing with shareholders, she has taken several courses to update her qualifications, notably in writing and investor relations. "You have to be able to read and write well, understand finances, and be able to explain the basic science that goes into our projects to do this job," she says.

However, a science background isn't a requirement for the job of investor relations manager, she says. A law background could be just as useful if not more, because of the legal matters preparation and submission of financial data involves.

An investor relations manager has to be able to coordinate major projects such as annual reports, and take responsibility for the final product.

Patience is an asset for this job. "You have to like dealing with people. If you think of the phone ringing as a interruption you'd be pretty unhappy with this job."

What is
the work like?

Jean works about 40 hours per week, but that can vary if there's an important deadline coming up. In that case, she works as many hours as necessary.

Her job as investor relations manager doesn't require much travel, except from her office in suburban Mississauga to investors' offices in downtown Toronto. Her working environment at the office is continually punctuated by telephone calls. She keeps her door open for anyone who might drop in, but most of her meetings are held in downtown Toronto.

▶By Ingrid Phaneuf   (09/98)

HEALTH

Investor Relations Manager
Sales and Marketing

■ What programme(s) I did:

B.Sc. in Genetics, University of Guelph, Ontario
B.Business Management/ Marketing, Ryerson Polytechnic University, Ontario

■ Average salary

$81 028

■ What are other routes to this positions?

Either a law degree or investor relations studies.

■ Skills and qualities you need for this job:

- need understanding of science and finance
- must be able to coordinate large projects
- must be able to meet deadlines and work well under pressure
- need writing and proof-reading skills

Photo : McMaster Photographers, Saskatoon

"The Seed Broker"

Aaron Mitchell is a marketing manager for Monsanto Canada inc.'s agricultural division. Usually, marketing means getting people to buy as much as possible, but the product that Aaron is trying to sell changes all the rules. Monsanto's product, a seed with genetically built in herbicide resistance reproduces itself! So while selling seeds to farmers, Aaron has to make sure they don't just use the seeds they buy to make more of their own. That would put Monsanto out of business.

What I do

Monsanto's product, called Roundup Ready Canola, is actually a growing system, a package of seeds and herbicide designed to work together to make high-yield crops. Monsanto scientists developed technology that allows them to add a gene to seeds, making them resistant to the chemicals used to kill weeds. They sell the herbicide and seeds together.

The problem is, once the genetically-altered seeds grow into a plant, its seeds still contain the gene responsible for herbicide resistance. Keeping clients from reproducing more seeds themselves isn't easy. And that's where Aaron comes in. As part of Monsanto's marketing strategy, Aaron organises special meetings where he explains Monsanto's technology to growers. At the same meetings, he explains to the farmers that they will have to sign an agreement not to use the crops they have grown as seed for the following year. Aaron has to make sure clients respect their agreement and are satisfied with the product.

Meanwhile, Aaron is also in contact with seed companies. Monsanto has an agreement with these firms too: they can use the DNA technology developed by Monsanto to grow the herbicide-resistant seeds, but only if they promise not to sell seeds to farmers who don't sign Monsanto's agreement.

"This is really the only way we can sell Roundup," says Aaron, who was one of the key players in developing Monsanto's marketing strategy.

The unique marketing approach requires a lot of one-on-one contact with farmers and seed companies. Aaron must be in constant contact with farmers, seed growers and plant breeders. He attends agricultural conventions and conferences across Canada, and sometimes even as far away as South America and Europe, to talk about Monsanto's product and listen to growers' concerns.

> **"You could come at what I'm doing now from a variety of backgrounds,"** says Aaron.

When he returns to the office, Aaron reports back on these meetings to company administrators. He also answers calls from growers and seed companies. And of course, he makes sure everyone who wants to use the product signs the agreement.

What skills
do I need?

Aaron has three degrees from the University of Saskatchewan: a B.Sc. in Chemistry, a B.Sc. in Agricultural Science, and a M.Sc. in Agriculture. "You could come at what I'm doing now from a variety of backgrounds," says Aaron. "For example, you could have a commerce degree, or a pure science degree." Aaron, who did not study commerce, says he got all his marketing training on the job.

Either way, Aaron says his most important job requirement is the ability to understand growers' concerns, and knowing what it takes to produce a variety of crops. He says listening skills are key to his job.

Aaron says a basic understanding of science and teaching skills (for the growers' meetings) are also needed in his job. A good business sense is also important, in order to assess which avenues of research might be profitable. And a knack for team work is essential. "We work on projects in teams, so you have to be able to see beyond your ego even if you think you're right about something."

What is
the work like?

Aaron works 60 hours a week, on the average. He spends half his time at the office. His office environment is fairly quiet. Most of his work there involves paperwork and phone calls. He also spends about 80 nights a year in hotels, attending conventions across Canada and sometimes overseas. Visits to growers and local seed company branches are also frequent.

He enjoys his job, and intends to stay involved with agriculture. "It's funny, because my father sold the farm and moved to the city when my two brothers and I were university-aged," says Aaron. "He wanted us to know there was a lot out there besides farming. But we all ended up involved with agriculture anyway. I guess you can take the boy off the farm, but you can't take the farm out of the boy."

▶By Ingrid Phaneuf   (09/98)

AGRICULTURE

Product Marketing Manager
Sales and Marketing

■ What programme(s) I did:

B.Sc. in Chemistry, U. of Saskatchewan, Saskatchewan
B.Sc in Agriculture, U. of Saskatchewan, Saskatchewan
M.Sc. in Agriculture, U. of Saskatchewan, Saskatchewan

■ Average salary

$77,272

■ What are other routes to this position?

A Business degree, with a good understanding of basic science and growing systems.

■ Skills and qualities you need for this job:

- must have understanding of growing systems and basic science
- need teaching skills
- must be good listener
- need a head for business and good sales skills

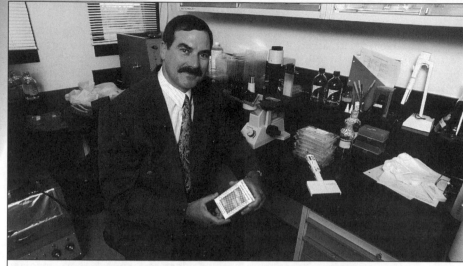

Photo : David Grandy Photography, Dartmouth

"Selling Seafood
Safety"

Raymond Roberts is helping to ensure the safety of the seafood that much of the world eats. Raymond is a sales manager at Jellett Inc., a company which produces diagnostic test kits to detect five toxins produced by sea algae. The toxins occur naturally in shellfish like oysters and clams, but can be deadly to humans.

What
I do

Raymond is responsible for promoting Jellett's diagnostic kits. These are foam coolers containing vials, staining solutions, sterilising liquid and chemical reagents - all ingredients and tools that shellfish processors can use to quickly and efficiently detect specific kinds of toxins.

Raymond's job is to find out where and to whom Jellett can sell them. "We have an international clientele, including government regulatory labs such as the Canadian Food Inspection Agency, and the aquaculture industry (including shellfish processors and harvesters). We have clients in the US, Europe, and the Far East, but I am always on the lookout for new business."

To find new customers, Raymond travels to aquaculture conferences and trade shows, reads literature on the shellfish industry, and talks with producers.

Raymond is also working on another challenge. Jellett's diagnostic kits are widely used, but have not yet been certified by an international body. Until the kits receive certification, selling them remains a challenge. Many processors are interested in the kits, but can't afford them. Normally, governments are willing to help fund companies to use tools like these to improve public health. However, without international certification, no government will provide funding. So Raymond is trying to convince governments across the world to fund processors to use the kits systematically.

Raymond spends a lot of time keeping on top of the certification issue. He researches newspaper clippings, television, the internet, computer databases, government publications and research journals, to monitor government regulations and attitudes, trends in the aquaculture research field and what competitors are up to.

What skills do I need?

Before working for Jellett, Raymond completed a Bachelor's in Biology, and a Master's in Business Administration (MBA). Both have proven necessary for his work. "My business training gives me an understanding of distribution — getting the product to the customer — and market research — how to gather information on new markets for our products. My scientific training comes in handy for understanding what our company does and how our product works, and explaining this to clients."

Raymond recommends that students who wish to work in biotech sales and marketing follow his example and obtain some mix of business and scientific training. The reason is simple: clients are usually experts in their field!

"In this field, a science background builds credibility. You're dealing with scientists who don't necessarily want to talk to a salesman. They want to talk to a professional who really knows what he's talking about. So you get more respect and more attention when you can defend your product on a scientific level."

Raymond says that persistence is key in his job, since he often has to overcome scepticism about the product. "It is a tough sell, because we haven't got certification yet. Clients say 'come back when you get certi-fication that the product does what you say it does'. We have scientific reports on the effectiveness of the tests, but people want to see that piece of paper proving our kits work."

Jellett expects to receive international certification for its kits in November from the Association of Official Analytical Chemists. "After certification, I still have to convince people our kits will save them money and are better than what they are using now."

What is the work like?

Raymond's job is more than a 9 to 5 commitment. "I usually work a 12-hour day, sometimes from 8 to 10. Sometimes I come in on weekends, when we have a problem to solve, or a deadline to meet."

Like many sales managers, Roberts is frequently on the road, going where potential customers are, and setting up demonstrations of Jellett's technology.

Roberts says a salesman must be prepared to have doors slammed in his face at times, and deal with both company and government red tape. "You have to keep at it, and understand that you'll get a lot of 'no's' before you get to a 'yes'. If you can persist despite this, and maintain a positive attitude, then you can be successful in marketing and sales in any field, biotech or any other."

▶By Wallie Seto and Sylvain Comeau (09/98)

AQUACULTURE

Sales Manager
Sales and Marketing

■ What programme(s) I did:

B.Sc. in Biology, St-Mary's University, Nova Scotia
M.B.A., St. Mary's University, Nova Scotia

■ Average salary

$48 000

■ What are other routes to this position?

A combination of science and business training at the university level.

■ Skills and qualities you need for this job:

- need to be a self-starter and self-motivator
- must have science and business background
- need strong people skills
- must be persistent

Photo : PPM Montreal

"Sold on Health"

Jean-François Raymond's job is helping doctors, nurses and pharmacists do theirs better. Jean-François is a sales representative at Schering Canada Inc., a large multinational pharmaceutical company with offices in more than 125 countries which manufactures a wide range of prescription drugs and over-the-counter products such as Claritin allergy pills, Dr. Scholl's foot powder and Coppertone sun tan lotion.

What I do

Jean-François' job is selling a medication called interferon, which has the brand name INTRON A. INTRON A (and all members of the interferon family) is actually a protein produced by the body: it induces healthy cells to manufacture an enzyme that helps fight a number of diseases such as some types of cancer and viral hepatitis. His sales territory covers much of Southwestern Quebec, from Sherbrooke to the Ottawa-Hull region.

To promote INTRON A, Jean-François calls regularly on specialists in hospitals. He makes the rounds of medical conventions and symposiums, attending five or six per year in Canada and the U.S., and he visits clients directly. On these visits he finds out what medicines doctors are interested in and explains his company's products to them.

Jean-François is also responsible for the follow-up service Schering offers to its clients. In most cases, he makes sure the medication is being used properly and informs clients of any new developments, reading any articles by doctors who have used Interferon.

> **"Credibility is important here. You're dealing with professionals on their level so you have to know what you're taking about."**

"I often meet with specialists, hospital pharmacists, nurses and sometime, family doctors to see how they're administering the medication. Some doctors don't know that our product can be used to treat a number of illnesses. It's my job to explain the versatility of INTRON A. If they're not using it, I try to convince them that it will help their patients."

After the sale and follow-up service, Jean-François writes up reports on his consulting

98

work, explaining to his bosses what needs to be done, how the client reacted and how the company's product performed. The company maintains long-term records so that it can follow up on work even years later.

What skills
do I need?

A sales representative for a pharmaceutical company such as Schering must have a science background, because he or she must be able to explain the technology behind the product. Most Schering sales reps have at least an undergraduate degree in the sciences. Jean-François has a Bachelor's and a Master's degree in microbiology.

"Credibility is important here. You're dealing with professionals on their level so you have to know what you're taking about. An education also helps you develop a good sense of judgement and organisation."

Honesty is a sales representative's best policy, according to Jean-François. "I'm not selling cars where I only see customers once and then that's it. I'm looking to build a long-term relationship, even a partnership. If clients ask me a question which I can't answer, I say so and tell them I'll get back to them later."

Jean-François says a sales rep should be disciplined, organised, have good work habits and be able to follow through on his promises. "I work on my own much of the time so it's important to have a good plan and to stick to it. There's a lot of competition in the pharmaceutical industry. If I don't fulfil my commitments as a supplier, the clients will simply go elsewhere.

What is
the work like?

Jean-François doesn't have a 9 to 5 routine. His work is often determined by the clients' availability and that often means working evenings and on weekends.

Jean-François also works as if he were his own boss, coming and going as he pleases, largely because he rarely sees his own supervisor. "I go into the office once a week, for about an hour, to get my mail. I see my boss even less often. But that doesn't mean I can take time off whenever I want to. I do have sales and promotional goals to take care of."

Jean-François also considers maintaining a strong, professional corporate image to be part of his job as a sales rep. " I'm the face of Schering. My job is to meet with customers, explain how INTRON A works and persuade them to use it on their patients. If I don't make a good impression on them, then our company won't convince the client to buy its products."

▶By Wallie Seto and Sylvain Comeau (09/98)

GETTING PRODUCTS OUT THERE

HEALTH

Sales Representative
Sales and Marketing

■ What programme(s) I did:

B.Sc. in Microbiology, University of Sherbrooke, Quebec
M.Sc. in Microbiology, University of Montreal, Quebec

■ Average salary

$45 000

■ What are other possible routes to this position?

A Bachelor of Commerce degree, a Nursing degree, or another Bachelor of Science degree

■ Skills and qualities you need for the job:

-need a science background
-must enjoy working independently
-must be a good listener
-need computer skills

"Watching out for Sales"

The pharmaceutical manufacturer Eli Lilly was the first company to produce insulin for people with diabetes using human genes, instead of extracting insulin from animals. Back in the early 1980s, the scientists at Eli Lilly inserted the human gene for insulin into the DNA of e-coli, a type of bacteria which proliferates rapidly. The result was the rapid production of human insulin. This was one of the discoveries that turned Eli Lilly into a North American leader among pharmaceutical companies, with offices in Canada and the United States. To coordinate sales operations across this large territory, Eli Lilly has regional sales directors like **Dawn Van Dam**.

Photo : Daniels & Gilonna Photography, Toronto

What I do

Dawn is responsible for all the sales operations in Ontario. She supervises the work of all the sales reps, continuing health education associates (the people who provide information about new Eli Lily products to doctors and other health professionals), and district sales managers in her region. And she keeps her boss, the vice-president of sales, up to date on all sales activities in Ontario.

Dawn has to keep track of everything the people in her sales region are doing, which means making a lot of phone calls on a regular basis.

Eli Lilly is growing fast and hiring a lot of new sales reps. It's Dawn's job to make sure there are enough sales representatives, and that they know what to do. She is not directly responsible for training, but she attends all sales meetings, meets with districts sales reps and educational specialists in order to keep on top of the sales process.

The biggest part of Dawn's job is to make sure her sales team carries out the sales strategy developed by the company's marketing department. Dawn has to keep track of everything the people in her sales region are doing, which means making a lot of phone calls on a regular basis. She also has to keep ongoing statistics on sales patterns across her region, and each sales rep's performance, a job which requires a lot of paperwork. And finally, she must ensure that her sales team doesn't go over budget.

Apart from her defined responsibilities, Dawn's specialised knowledge of her region often comes in handy at Eli Lilly. For instance, Dawn or other regional sales managers often know of well-known doctors in their regions who might be interested in getting involved in clinical trials on products already on the market, trials on humans done for marketing reasons. The sales director might suggest a doctor simply because his or her involvement could give the trial better publicity.

What skills
do I need?

Mathematical skills are essential to Dawn's job, because a regional sales director has to be able to interpret statistics about her reps' performance and market research information, and keep track of profits and expenses. Organisational skills are also key. Dawn has to be able to keep track of many people at the same time.

A regional sales director needs finely developed people skills. Dawn has to deal with all kinds of people, and with all kinds of problems every day. She has to be able to be tough when a sales rep isn't performing. "You can't just let people walk all over you," she says.

At the same time, Dawn has to be able to motivate people. A regional sales director has to be a good leader who people trust. "You have to be a good coach, and a team player," she says. And to be all these things at once, she says, you need a lot of energy and must never neglect to follow up on problems and find solutions when necessary.

What is
the work like?

Dawn works long hours: from 8:30 a.m. to 5 p.m. weekdays, and then weekday evenings from 9 p.m. to 11:30 p.m. She doesn't work Friday nights, but makes up for lost time by working on Sunday nights instead. At night she keeps track of her email and returns phone calls. During the day she works on data analysis and meets with people over the phone or in person.

She divides her time between her home office and her office at Eli Lilly.

When she has to analyse data and make phone calls, she works at home. When she has to meet with people in person, she goes to the office. "I have two kids and a husband, so between 5 p.m. and 9 p.m. I spend time with them," she says.

At home, her work environment is quiet, except for the constant stream of phone meetings.

At home, her work environment is quiet, except for the constant stream of phone meetings. She only goes into the office for appointments, so interruptions there are rare.

Dawn likes her job, and plans to stay with the company. "This field is constantly growing and changing, and that creates a lot of opportunities," she says.

▶By Ingrid Phaneuf   (09/98)

GETTING PRODUCTS OUT THERE

HEALTH

Senior Sales Executive
Sales and Marketing

■ What programme(s) I did:

B.Business Adminstration, Wharton Business School, U.S.A.

■ Average salary

$116 998

■ What are other routes to this position?

Undergraduate and Master's degrees in business administration and marketing.

■ Skills and qualities you need for this job:

- need leadership skills
- need mathematical and analytical skills
- must be energetic
- must have good organisational, time-management skills

101

"Joining Forces"

Sometimes size isn't everything. A big bio-pharmaceutical company like Pasteur Merieux Connaught, which has its own research and development branch and manufactures, markets and distributes its own products, still needs help from smaller companies. The reason? Smaller companies often have excellent ideas and have carried out research that larger companies haven't. On the other hand, smaller companies often don't have the resources to market and distribute products on their own.

Pasteur Merieux Conaught is always on the lookout for promising partners. As Strategic Alliances Manager at Pasteur Merieux Conaught, **Duncan Jones**' job is finding them, then making sure all the steps involved in setting up a partnership run smoothly.

What I do

Duncan specialises in developing partnerships with university researchers. When Pasteur Merieux decided to develop a medication for inner-ear infections, Duncan set out to find the best researchers in the field. "A lot of the time, university researchers start up a project and want someone else to finish it," says Duncan. "Big companies like ours might be interested because the researchers' technology compliments ours."

A large part of the strategic alliances manager's job is keeping abreast of research at different universities across Canada and the U.S. Duncan makes a lot of phone calls and reads researchers' articles in many scientific journals. He also travels to conventions and conferences to meet with researchers and get to know them and their work.

Duncans' job also involves making his company appear accessible to and interested in researchers. "Because Pasteur Merieux Connaught is a big, well-known company, the person in charge of strategic alliances doesn't have to call on smaller companies most of the time — they call us," explains Duncan. "But researchers still have to see us as the easiest company to deal with."

It is important for the strategic alliances manager to be familiar with the history and financial situation of the company he's dealing with.

Duncan spends a large portion of his working time negotiating legal agreements with researchers and smaller companies. Finding researchers and negotiating a deal can take anywhere from six months to three years. The terms of an agreement vary from one company to another. Some research companies may need financing to complete their research, while others may not. It is important for the strategic alliances manager to be familiar with the history and financial situation of the company he's dealing with.

After making agreements between his and smaller companies, Duncan must make sure both parties keep their end of the deal. "You have to make sure you make your payments on time," says Duncan. "And you have to ensure good relations with partner companies, so if you miss a payment you won't be facing a lawsuit right away."

Of course, company executives must approve all agreements. The strategic alliances manager has to keep keep his boss (usually a vice-president) up to date on new and interesting research, and advise him or her on partnerships which could pay off for the company.

What skills
do I need?

Duncan has an M.A. in Pure Sciences and an M.BA. from the University of Toronto. "Overall knowledge of science is useful when it comes to talking to researchers, and a business background helps in general planning and management," he says. "Financial knowledge also helps when you have to make decisions about investing in smaller companies."

But Duncan says there are alternative training paths to a career in strategic alliances. He says a lot of strategic alliances and business development people have some training in law — which is very useful when it comes to negotiating business agreements.

Communications and negotiation skills, and the ability to juggle a lot of financial and legal obligations to different partners are all important qualities in a strategic alliances manager. "There are always several deals being considered, or in the works," says Duncan.

What is
the work like?

Being a strategic alliances manager involves a lot of travelling to conferences to meet researchers. Because Pasteur Merieux Connaught is an international company, these employees travel to many countries.

The average work week is about 45 hours, not including travelling time, and not counting a lot of reading in the evening to keep track of the latest research developments.

In Duncan's case, a mix of internal and external activities means that no two days are the same. "The person currently responsible for strategic alliances has been away at conventions for three weeks straight now," says Duncan. So while the strategic alliances manager's work may be hard, meeting researchers in many different fields makes for a fascinating career.

▶By Ingrid Phaneuf   (09/98)

HEALTH

Strategic Alliances Manager
Sales and Marketing

■ What programme(s) I did:

B.Sc in Biochemistry and Chemistry, University of Toronto, Ontario
M.Sc. in Biochemistry, University of Toronto, Ontario
M.BA., University of Toronto, Ontario

■ Average salary

$60 000

■ What are other routes to this position?

A degree in law, combined with at least a basic understanding of science.

■ Skills and qualities you need for this job:

- need communications skills
- must have scientific and business knowledge
- must have ability to negotiate
- requires some financial knowledge

"The Negotiator"

Photo : David Grandy Photography, Dartmouth

Donna Viger is a lawyer who has leapt into biotechnology. Instead of arguing cases in court, she puts her negotiating and analytical skills to work for the Institute for Marine Biosciences, a research laboratory in Halifax. When scientists at the laboratory work with biotech companies, they ask Donna to write a contract spelling out what work has to be done, who is responsible for which jobs and who owns the end results.

What I do

In the biotechnology field, a research centre such as the Institute for Marine Biosciences often works alongside scientists from other institutes or private companies. However, before the work begins, each side must know which tasks they are responsible for and who owns any discoveries made during the experiments. Sometimes, the discoveries made in a lab —for example, a new painkiller — can later be marketed and sold for large profits. Therefore, before a collaborative project begins, the people involved will sit down with a lawyer, like Donna, to draft a contract.

When she is writing a contract, she'll ask the scientists involved in the project to explain what they're doing and why, in simple terms.

It's a job Donna particularly enjoys. Writing contracts involves listening carefully to all sides, understanding what people want from a project and helping them come up with compromises when disagreements arise. It is, she adds, "a challenge."

When Donna isn't negotiating and drafting contracts, she is responsible for other writing projects. Each year, the Institute publishes a "performance report" explaining all the different kinds of projects the Institute has worked on that year. It's up to Donna to get that information from the Institute's directors and scientists and to write the report. She also prepares ads describing the Institute's work for publication in trade and business magazines as well as newspapers.

What skills do I need?

Unlike most people at the Institute, Donna does not have a science degree. She majored in political science at the University of New Brunswick before going on to do her law degree. After four years in law practice, she realised she no longer wanted to do it.

"They were concerned that I didn't have a science background," she says. "But my writing and analytical skills got me the job."

She worked at a couple of jobs unrelated to law before seeing an ad for her current job.

The Institute was looking for someone with a B.Sc. plus a law degree or an MBA. Donna had only the law degree but applied anyway. "They were concerned that I didn't have a science background," she says. "But my writing and analytical skills got me the job."

Since then, she's learned plenty about science by asking questions. "You gain a certain expertise by talking with people," she says. When she is writing a contract, she'll ask the scientists involved in the project to explain what they're doing and why, in simple terms. And she keeps asking questions until she understands.

> **"You need thinking skills, people skills, management skills. These aren't taught formally but they are sometimes more valuable than what you learn in school."**

To create and write contracts, Donna says, "negotiating skills are very valuable." She has to listen carefully to what people involved in an experiment want, come up with compromises when disagreements arise and write everything down in a clear, understandable way.

"Your formal education is only one half of what you need on a job," she adds. "You need thinking skills, people skills, management skills. These aren't taught formally but they are sometimes more valuable than what you learn in school."

What is the work like?

Donna arrives at the Institute, located on the Dalhousie University campus, at 8:30 a.m. She has her own office which is essential, she says, especially when she's working on a contract. "I need to be able to close my door and think." She'll check her email and telephone messages but after that she sets her priorities for the day.

While her work day officially ends at 5:00 p.m., Donna says "I work a fair number of extra hours." Every two or three months, she attends biotechnology conferences elsewhere in Canada. She also travels to Ottawa to meet with other business programme managers at research institutes across Canada.

Donna admits working with scientists can be "intimidating" since she doesn't have a science background. However, she doesn't let her fear stand in the way of doing her job. "I'll never know as much as they do, but I have to know enough to do my job. And people here are quite willing to sit and work with you to give you that information" she says. "They understand that I bring value to the Institute and that together, we're greater than the sum of our parts."

▶By Liz Warwick   (09/98)

AQUACULTURE

Business Programme Manager
Administration and Regulation

■ What programme(s) I did:

B.A. in Political Science, University of New Brunswick, New Brunswick
LL.B, University of New Brunswick, New Brunswick

■ Average salary

$50 000

■ What are other routes to this position?

To become a manager of business programmes, a B.Sc. and an MBA or a law degree are required.

■ Skills and qualities you need for this job:

- must have a knowledge of science
- need strong organisational skills
- must have the ability to write clearly and precisely
- must enjoy negotiating

105

"The Pharmaceutical King"

In 1986, **Dr. Francesco Bellini** was working as head of the Biochemicals Division for Institut Armand-Frappier, a Montreal-area research institute. He enjoyed his job but was surprised at how little research was being commercialised. "I thought really good science was done in Canada but it was not being exploited," he says. "It was being done at universities and institutes and hospitals, but nobody was making a profit from it." So Bellini co-founded BioChem Pharma Inc., a company that has become one of Quebec's leading biotechnology companies.

What I do

As his title of chief executive officer (CEO) suggests, Bellini holds the ultimate responsibility BioChem Pharma. He decides, in consultation with other company members, how much money will be spent on research and development. He decides which companies BioChem Pharma will work with to develop and market new drugs. At the end of the year, it is Bellini who must explain to people who have invested money in the company (the shareholders) why the company has made or lost money.

It's a tough job but one that Bellini relishes. He co-founded the company in 1986 and has seen BioChem Pharma grow from five people to over 1 000 employees. The company makes 3TC, one of the most successful drugs available for treating HIV/AIDS. BioChem Pharma is developing drugs to treat cancer and hepatitis B, has created vaccines against various diseases including the flu. It also sells kits to test for allergies and infectious diseases like tuberculosis.

Photo : Courtesy of BioChem Pharma

A CEO sets both long-term and short-term goals for his or her company. For Bellini, that means making sure the company is constantly developing new products. "You have to make sure your pipeline is always full," he says. "Then you know where you'll be five years from now." To keep the "pipeline full," Bellini depends on his research scientists to think about new products and propose ways to make those products a reality.

Bellini (working with other company members) also negotiates "strategic alliances" or partnerships with companies in order to share ideas, knowledge and resources. These alliances have been key to BioChem's success, allowing the company to develop and market new products at a very fast pace. One of the most important partnerships has been with the large British pharmaceutical company Glaxo Wellcome, which markets 3TC around the world.

What skills do I need?

A CEO needs strong persuasive skills, particularly when a company is starting up. "When we started this company, people were very sceptical about the future of biotechnology," Bellini says. He convinced investors to put money into the company. He also built, and continues to build, a team of people he felt shared the company's vision. "You cannot work alone. You need the organisation," he says. "You make your vision a reality through people."

Bellini demands that his employees always be straight with him. If a research project is running late or isn't yielding the expected results, Bellini says he needs to know.

A CEO, adds Bellini, must always be willing to listen to the company's employees. When he meets with other company executives to talk about BioChem Pharma's future, Bellini sometimes has to change his ideas. "You realise that their idea is right and your idea is wrong. You have to have the courage to change your mind," he says.

Bellini demands that his employees always be straight with him. "I don't like surprises," he says in a firm quiet voice. If a research project is running late or isn't yielding the expected results, Bellini says he needs to know. Since he deals with where the company is going in the future, Bellini must have an accurate, detailed picture of BioChem Pharma's current state. People who don't understand this, he adds, don't last long at the company.

What is
the work like?

Bellini quite naturally has his own office which overlooks landscaped grounds of the BioChem Pharma building. However, he doesn't spend much time in the office. His day often starts very early with breakfast meetings or presentations to business groups. He often travels both in Canada and around the world to meet with potential investors and work on developing partnerships.

Bellini's day never ends at 5:00 p.m. If he's not at a dinner meeting, then he might be organising fund-raising events for the Canadian Cancer Society, the Heart and Stroke Foundation or the Montreal Museum of Contemporary Art. He also serves on various Boards of Directors including Molson Companies Ltd., North American Vaccine Inc. and the Italian Chamber of Commerce.

Bellini's approach to his job is straightforward. "You have to be committed to the company and committed to the shareholders," he says. "And you have to be honest with yourself. Don't try to sell something that you don't have."

▶By Liz Warwick   (09/98)

HEALTH

Chief Executive Officer
Administration and Regulation

■ What programme(s) I did:

B.Sc. in Chemistry, Loyola College (now Concordia University), Quebec
Ph.D. in Organic Chemistry, University of New Brunswick, New Brunswick

■ Average salary

$159 806

■ What are other routes to this position?

Ph.D. in science along with years of management experience.

■ Skills and qualities you need for this job:

- have knowledge of science and finance
- be willing to take risks
- be an excellent negotiator
- be willing to spend many years on a project

107

"Protecting the Goat"

Photo : Patrick Villeneuve, Montreal

Dana Rath is Nexia Biotechnologies' legal and financial guru. He deals with investors and regulatory bodies, sees that his company is properly insured, and keeps an eye on Nexia's competitors so his firm's scientists can concentrate on research and development. "I envision myself as the guard on a stagecoach. The stagecoach is racing forward and I look backwards", he says, referring to how he protects Nexia with contracts and patents.

What I do

Nexia Biotechnologies is a small biotech company that recently found a way to make goat milk into a source of human proteins used for medication. Although the proteins in this case are still secret, drugs that could be produced using this technology include a growth hormone used to treat patients undergoing chemotherapy, insulin for diabetes and blood clotting agents for hemophiliacs.

The real breakthrough? Nexia recently succeeded in creating a goat that produces the human protein in its own milk! First scientists at Nexia modified a human gene to produce protein only in the mammary gland. Then they inserted this modified gene into a goat embryo. Willow — Canada's first transgenic goat — was born in August 1998. Scientists will be able to extract the desired proteins from her milk to make a drug for humans.

But there's more: Breeding this goat, called a "founder animal," will result in a herd of animals with milk containing human protein — in other words, a cheaper, easier way to manufacture human drugs. But it will take at least five years after Willow's birth before such a drug can be sold.

Dana also obtains patents for products, fills out regulatory board paperwork, negotiates leases, and buys goat insurance — a task more daunting than it might sound.

Until then, Nexia relies on venture capitalist investors and corporate partners to finance its research. Dana's job is to keep all parties happy while protecting Nexia's interests. As part owners, investors sit on Nexia's board of directors where Dana takes minutes and prepares resolutions. He also draws up financial statements showing investors how their money is spent and oversees bill payments to make sure board resolutions are carried out. To satisfy corporate partners hiring Nexia to develop specific products, Dana prepares contracts and agreements guaranteeing secrecy and results.

Dana also obtains patents for products, fills out regulatory board paperwork, negotiates leases, and buys goat insurance — a task more daunting than it might sound. Although each initial goat Nexia works with is worth about a thousand dollars, a founder goat's value can reach $15 million! Dana had to find a suitable insurance policy taking effect upon the founder's birth. Quite a challenge!

What skills
do I need?

Dana has always had varied interests. As an undergraduate, he completed a Bachelor's in science, majoring in psychology. Then he did a law degree, but after articling and passing the bar, felt drawn to business. After two years of courses and another two years auditing companies for the major accounting firm Ernst and Young, he became a certified Chartered Accountant. After a few more years in accounting, he moved to pharmaceutical giant Abbott Laboratories. That was when he heard about a job at Nexia.

The scientists who run Nexia were looking for an in-house accountant, but also wanted someone to explain legal matters — Dana Rath's exact skill set. "When I met with Nexia for the first time," explains Dana, "management said; 'We don't understand when lawyers talk to us and need someone who can explain these things to us.'"

Dana's legal training — which taught him how to see both sides of an argument — has come in handy in other ways. "I report to the president, represent the employees and report to the shareholders. I have to be able to voice all positions."

What is
the work like?

The light on Dana's telephone is always lit and he has to return many messages, but he doesn't have a routine. "One of the nice things about my job is that it's not at all repetitive on a day-to-day basis. On a monthly basis, there are things that always come up, like making sure the financial statements are correct and analysing them. Twice a month, I have to monitor our investments, reinvest and predict our cash needs for the next three months. Other than that, things come ad hoc."

Dana usually works from 9 until 6:30, although it gets busier before board meetings. He's also been spending time pondering Nexia's plans to become a publicly-traded company. Sometimes, he works until two or three a.m..

"No one is telling me that I have to work until three in the morning to produce something, but it's my responsibility. If something needs to be done, I'll do whatever it takes to get it done."

▶By Tracey Arial   (09/98)

HEALTH

Chief Financial Officer
Administration and Regulation

■ What programme(s) I did:

B.Sc. in Psychology, McGill University, Quebec
LL.B (Law) degree, University of Ottawa, Ontario
Graduate Diploma in Public Accountancy, McGill University, Quebec
Registered Chartered Accountant

■ Average salary

$127 900

■ What are other routes to this position?

Any combination of finance, law and business experience.

■ Skills and qualities you need for this job:

- must be able to understand and present financial information
- must have detail-oriented thinking
- need business experience
- need to be a leader

"Taking Biotech to the Public"

Take an onion and crush it. What do you get? At a place called SABIC (Saskatchewan Agricultural Biotechnology Information Centre), by adding a few simple ingredients, you get the onion's DNA. The onion-crushing experiment is part of SABIC's programme to educate people about biotechnology. The person who runs it is **Lisa Jategaonkar**. She's a woman with a mission: to make biotechnology understandable to ordinary people.

What
I do

Lisa was hired in 1997 by Ag-West Biotech, a non-profit group in Saskatchewan aiming to educate people about the uses and benefits of biotechnology in agriculture. Her first task was to start up SABIC.

"The SABIC lab is designed to give people a chance to actually see what biotechnology is all about," Lisa says. "We want to change biotechnology from something that is very mysterious and boring to something that is a bit more commonplace."

To start up SABIC, Lisa met with scientists and university professors involved in agri-cultural biotechnology. She asked them about important issues and ideas for the lab to show. Then Lisa began thinking up experiments that would help people understand these ideas. One experiment allows people to use gel electrophoresis, a technique to separate cut pieces of DNA which scientists commonly use to isolate specific genes and trace genetic diseases. In the experiment, DNA is placed on a gel-like substance and given an electrical charge. Because the DNA is stained, a viewer can actually see how it breaks up into different sized fragments.

SABIC officially opened October 1997. When a group wants to visit SABIC, Lisa calls upon her "demonstrators", graduate students who conduct the experiments and answer people's questions. She arranges tours and makes sure the lab is ready to go. Lisa is also responsible for writing and updating SABIC fact sheets (called "Any Questions?"), which are information pamphlets available to the public.

Lisa is currently working on a newsletter to be sent to grocery stores which will help grocers answer consumer questions about the impact of biotechnology on food. For example, people sometimes wonder about the safety of eating a genetically-altered fruit — like a strawberry altered to grow more easily in cold climates. The newsletter is designed to give clear answers to such concerns.

What skills
do I need?

Lisa holds a B.Sc. and a M.Sc. in Food Biotechnology. Because she works closely with scientists and other experts, she finds having a graduate degree helpful. "It gives you a lot of credibility dealing with scientists," she says.

As part of her job, Lisa travels to conferences and trade shows, meets with school teachers and sometimes talks with politicians about biotechnology issues. To effectively communicate her ideas, she draws on her public-speaking skills, honed by years of participation in debate clubs. It's also important, she adds, to be a good listener. People often come into SABIC with questions, fears or doubts about biotechnology. It's part of Lisa's job to make sure they get the answers they need.

The field of biotechnology is rapidly changing and Lisa says it is important to stay on top of new research and issues. She often uses the Internet to research what's happening in the field or to find answers to questions people have asked. She also uses her computer to design presentations (graphs and other visual aids) for groups interested in agricultural biotechnology.

What is
the work like?

Lisa arrives at her office about 8:00 a.m. If a tour is scheduled that day, she'll pop next door to SABIC's premises and see that the lab has all supplies required for the demonstrations. She also makes sure there are enough fact sheets available.

Another part of her job is to keep changing the lab's experiments and displays. Often young people will visit the lab several times — once as a field trip, another time with their family, etc. So Lisa needs to keep updating and changing the lab. Lisa also meets regularly with educational, agricultural and public awareness groups to talk about ways to inform the public about ag-biotech issues.

About once a month, Lisa travels to a trade show or a conference where she presents information on agricultural biotechnology. Most of the travel is within Saskatchewan. Lisa also meets regularly with the SABIC advisory board (the people who worked with her to set up the lab) to talk about SABIC's progress and share ideas on how the lab is run.

For Lisa, one of the great joys of her job is the variety of work she handles. From thinking up new experiments to writing a newsletter, there's never a dull moment, she says. "Every day is a new project and a new responsibility."

►By Liz Warwick   (09/98)

AGRICULTURE

Communications Manager

Administration and Regulation

■ What programme(s) I did:

B.Sc. in Food Biotechnology, University of Ottawa, Ontario
M.Sc. in Food Biotechnology, University of Saskatchewan, Saskatchewan

■ Average salary

$35 000

■ What are other routes to this position?

An undergraduate degree in science and probably a Master's degree in either Science or Biotechnology. Public relations or communications would advisable.

■ Skills and qualities you need for this job:

- need excellent writing and public speaking skills
- must be able to use different computer software progr.
- must enjoy the challenge of making science and biotechnology accessible to public
- should enjoy meeting and talking with people

111

Photo : PPM, Montreal

"Holding the Purse Strings"

Even a company performing tasks as sophisticated as genetic cloning needs someone to watch the purse strings. At BioSignal, **Lucie St-Georges**, controller and vice president of finance, is the one who keeps tabs on financial affairs. "The president is the visionary; he's the one who plots our strategy and our mission. But I'm the one who makes the president's vision happen. I tell him that a particular project is costing us too much, or that we need $5 million for it instead of $4 million."

What I do

BioSignal produces tools pharmaceutical companies use for drug screening, the preliminary tests conducted to measure a drug's safety and effectiveness before human or animal testing. BioSignal may be hired, for instance, to clone a particular bacteria or virus, or human cells which a company will use to see how a particular drug functions "in vitro" — in the test tube.

Lucie is not a scientist herself, but a certified accountant. She's responsible for forecasting, budgeting, and evaluating her company's value; she makes sure employees are working on budget, supervising the company's four accountants. When the president says what he wants, she decides whether it is possible.

Lucie's work as a controller involves handling her company's cash flow: she makes sure that suppliers are paid only once for products, that clients pay for services rendered and that employees get paid. Lucie also monitors internal control systems designed to make sure that the company's money is put to good use and not stolen or defrauded. "I'm the one who makes sure the company runs smoothly," says Lucie.

Lucie says people skills are crucial to her job.

The controller does a lot more than just number crunching, however. Lucie is responsible for rounding up funding for BioSignal's research and development . She applies to government funding agencies for grants and loans, which cover about 50 per cent of the company's R&D expenses. "I learn everything about the operations of this and other companies, because I deal with the President and C.F.O. of companies that we have partnerships with, or with whom we're negotiating a deal."

What skills
do I need?

Lucie's career path started with nine years of work at Chartered Accountancy firm Price Waterhouse. She became interested in technology while working as a controller at a software company. "I got into the biotech field because I have extensive knowledge of the high-tech industry, the taxation related to R&D, and the government departments which provide funding to companies."

Lucie says people skills are crucial to her job. She has a very hands-off management style. "I'm very demanding; the employees know that they can't screw up. But if they do their work and deliver, I won't bother them. I give them a lot of leeway, because I need their trust. It seems to work, because one fellow I worked with at the last company followed me to this one."

Biotech is also a high risk, uncertain field; Lucie says that being a decision maker in that environment requires an ability to take risks. "You can't be sure if you made the right decision until a year or two later, when you see the result. In the end, you make the decision that feels right, after weighing the pros and cons."

Lucie says the ability to learn from mistakes is crucial. A bad decision at a software company she once worked for cost most of management, including her, their jobs. "Just because you make a mistake, it doesn't mean you're not good at what you do. You will make mistakes sometimes. Instead of wasting time and energy on regret, you should just try not to repeat them."

What is
the work like?

Lucie normally works 45 hours per week. Her day starts reading magazines and newsletters covering the biotech industry, checking her mail and replying to queries. Afternoons usually involve meetings. These have recently involved discussing expansion and hiring new employees with the president and vice president. She also spends time preparing for seminars and presentations at business conferences. Sometimes she even handles immigration matters for new employees.

The work is more intense at certain times of year, such as at the end of the company's fiscal year (when the company must make accounting reports to the government), when she works 10 hours a day.

Keeping up to date with the industry is an important part of her job, Lucie says. "There's always new technology, and plenty of deals going on in the industry. It's a fast changing industry, and we have to be aware of the changing environment around us."

▶By Wallie Seto and Sylvain Comeau (09/98)

HEALTH

Controller
Administration and Regulation

■ What programme(s) I did:

B.A.A., University of Quebec at Montreal (UQAM), Quebec
Chartered Accountancy designation.

■ Average salary

$81 739

■ What are other routes to this position?

An advanced business degree, such as an M.B.A.

■ Skills and qualities you need for this job:

- need business background.
- must have ability to manage small or large groups
- computer skills are essential
- should enjoy working in a fast-paced, fast-changing environment

"Watching over the Flock"

Catherine Sutter is director of human resources for Kinetek Pharmaceuticals, a company that develops new drugs for manageable and chronic diseases such as cancer and diabetes. Since Kinetek Pharmaceuticals is a research and development company, most of its employees are scientists. Catherine Sutter keeps operations running smoothly by keeping employees happy and well-informed, and by dealing with any problems. She keeps the company's Senior Vice-President of Finance and Administration up to date on her work and employees' performance.

What I do

Even before new employees join Kinetek, Catherine is dealing with them, attending interviews for new full-time positions and checking the references of potential candidates.

When employees join the company, she is on hand to welcome them on their first day with an armload of forms and all the information they need to get started. She has to make sure new employees are aware of their health coverage (Kinetek provides a full medical plan, including eye and dental care, plus life and disability insurance). She also makes sure they sign promises to keep the company's research projects secret (called confidentiality agreements).

Then she gives them tax and benefit forms to fill out, and assigns security cards and keys as required. She also informs them of corporate policies on work hours, on safety practices and building security policies, and she allocates desk and lab space. She also responds to job inquiries, which come in on a daily basis, and organises social events such as barbecues and Christmas parties.

Catherine sees that everyone gets paid and is responsible for grievances made by unhappy employees. She says she's never had to deal with a grievance yet, but the solution could involve moving an employee to another department or even recommending that an employee be fired. Catherine may also counsel an employee who has been laid off or fired. As the number of employees increases, she says, so do the number of problems.

The human resources manager also develops longer-term projects for employees' benefit. One of Catherine's current projects is a review of salary scales at Kinetek Pharmaceuticals. She is doing research on pay scales in force for employees with similar jobs at other companies, in order to make sure the salaries Kinetek is offering are competitive.

Catherine is presently at work on an employee incentive programme. She is trying to come up with ways to reward hard-working employees and develop their pride in their work. She is also trying to complete an employee manual which will contain all the forms and information she gives new employees, as well as more detailed information about company policy on leaves of absence, sexual harassment, pay schedules, and so on.

What skills
do I need?

Catherine didn't study to become a human resources manager. In fact, her university education was in sciences (she has a B.Sc. in biochemistry). She says her scientific background does make it easier for her to relate to employees at Kinetek Pharmaceuticals, most of whom are scientists.

Catherine learned her managerial skills when she worked as an office manager at a shark fishery in Alabama, and later, when she worked as lab manager at the University of British Columbia.

Good planning and communication skills are essential to the work of a human resources manager. Having initiative and being able to work independently are also crucial, Catherine says. "I'm not in a team with other people working on the same project. My team is the whole company."

What is
the work like?

The human resources manager spends about 80 per cent of her time at work at her desk. The rest is spent meeting with supervisors and employees, and interviewing new employees. Catherine's supervisor (the Senior VP) lives in Ontario, so she reports to him when she sees him, about once every month. The rest of the time, it's up to her to do her job on her own.

Her work environment is generally quiet, and her hours are regular — about 40 per week, unless there's some kind of deadline to meet and she has to work on the weekend. But that's rare. Research scientists tend to keep late hours, and the company is pretty flexible about employees' schedules. But as human resources manager, it's important for Catherine to be at the office during the regular work day. "In this position I have to be at the office for at least five core hours of the day to deal with people who work during regular office hours," she says.

▶By Ingrid Phaneuf   (09/98)

HEALTH

Human Resources Manager
Administration and Regulation

■ **What programme(s) I did:**

B.Sc. in Biochemistry, University of Victoria, British Colombia

■ **Average salary**

$69 231

■ **What are other routes to this position?**

Degree in human resources management is advisable, or a B.Sc..

■ **Skills and qualities you need for this job:**

- must have strong computer skills
- need "people" skills
- must have good management skills
- must be able to work independently

"The Legal Eagle"

Photo : Brian Gould Photography, Winnipeg

Ever wondered what the difference is between the Tylenol in the yellow and red bottle, and the similar pain reliever in the plain white bottle? It might not be much — a matter of an ingredient or two, maybe just something to relieve allergy symptoms — but **Dr. Leo Wong** could probably tell you. Dr. Wong is manager of Intellectual Property for the pharmaceutical company Cangene. His job is to make sure Cangene's drugs are different from other similar products on the market, so his company can manufacture and market its drugs without being taken to court by a competitor. He also makes sure Cangene's own original drugs are legally protected.

What I do

A company that discovers or creates a drug in Canada has patent protection for the drug for about 20 years, meaning that during that period, nobody else can use their recipe as a basis for developing another similar drug. After that, companies can create similar drugs based on the same recipe, but first, they must be different. Cangene is both creating drugs based on other companies drugs, called "generic" drugs and creating their own from scratch, known as "brand-name" drugs. So they have to make sure nobody copies their brand-name drugs, and that their generic drugs are different enough from similar drugs to avoid a lawsuit. Dealing with proprietary issues for both kinds of drugs is Dr. Wong's responsibility. "I'm an offense and a defence player at the same time," he says.

When a scientist at Cangene develops a generic drug, he or she checks with Dr. Wong to make sure the drug developed is in fact new. This is particularly important because brand-name manufacturers frequently try to take generic drug manufacturers to court. When a scientist creates a name-brand drug, the process is the same.

In order to give his colleagues answers right away, Dr. Wong must keep up to date on the all the latest developments in the pharmaceutical industry. He does this by reading scientific journals and checking developments on the Internet. He is also in constant communication with his company's lawyers in order to keep up with the latest laws on intellectual property. He has to know when one of Cangene's products could provoke a lawsuit, particularly in the United States, where intellectual property laws are much stricter than in Canada.

Throughout this entire process, Dr. Wong must keep Cangene's administrators up to date on whether the company's drugs threaten the intellectual property rights of other companies. This involves writing regular reports.

What skills do I need?

Dr. Wong has a Ph.D. In Pharmacology from the University of Manitoba, as well as an MBA from the University of Manitoba. His job requires a science/ business administration training so that he can work and communicate well with scientists, lawyers, and company administrators. He needs to be able to understand the research and development process as well as business and legal considerations.

Dr. Wong says he'll deal with several things in the same day, and his ability to drop what he's doing to deal with an emergency (like a possible lawsuit) is key.

Analytical and problem-solving skills are very important to his job. When Dr. Wong finds out a drug being developed by a Cangene scientist is in danger of violating another company's intellectual property rights, he often suggests an alternative way to make the drug, or an additional ingredient that would make it more legally viable. "You have to be able to look at the big picture, and not just focus on one little thing," says Dr. Wong.

Versatility and flexibility are also important to Dr. Wong's job, as is the ability to man-age time. Dr. Wong says he'll deal with several things in the same day, and his ability to drop what he's doing to deal with an emergency (like a possible lawsuit) is key. "Priorities change constantly throughout a single day," he says.

What is the work like?

Dr. Wong says he works about 60 hours per week on average. His work day begins at around 7:30 a.m. and ends at 6:30 p.m. at the latest. On weekends he spends time trekking to libraries and reading the latest scientific journals, when he isn't spending time with his family.

Dr. Wong's working environment tends to be quiet — he has his own office near one of the research labs. When he's not meeting with lawyers, research scientists, or company higher-ups he's busy looking for the latest information on the Web, or in scientific journals.

Dr. Wong loves his job. "Not too many other jobs provide the same opportunity to be exposed to so many areas of science at once," he says. "I really like to be able to see the forest and not just the individual leaves."

►By Ingrid Phaneuf   (09/98)

HEALTH

Intellectual Property Manager

Administration and Regulation

■ **What programme(s) I did:**

Ph.D. in Pharmacology, U. of Manitoba, Manitoba
M.BA. (Masters' in Business Administration) ,
University of Manitoba, Manitoba

■ **Average salary**

$66 667

■ **What are other routes to this position?**

In biotechnology, a science degree is usually required, but people interested in getting into intellectual property management can also do it through training in business administration, and a law degree. Usually a combination of science and law training is the best.

■ **Skills and qualities you need for this job:**

- need an understanding of research and development
- must have computer skills
- need an understanding of patent, trademark, and copyright laws
- must be able to work independently
- need good communication skills

"The Science Scribe"

Photo : Daniels & Gilonna Photography, Toronto

Since she began writing about science, **Stephanie Yanchinski** has been driven by the need to make the complex seem simple. "When people say: 'You explained something I didn't understand,' that gives me the most tremendous buzz." As a science journalist, Stephanie writes articles to explain biotechnology to the public.

What I do

Born and raised in Montreal, Stephanie now works at her home office in Toronto, where she settled in 1987 after living in Europe and Asia. As a science writer in biotechnology, she has to explain technical terms in plain English. She has to digest the complex information coming out of the industry and put it into simpler words for the public. "I think the Canadian public wants to read more about science," she says. "People want to understand what's going on around them. It's natural."

Stephanie also puts her writing and communications skills to use as a communications strategist, helping companies reach the public, governments and other companies by planning and producing clear and interesting documents (newsletters, reports, reviews, etc.). Some of her many clients include Glaxo Wellcome and Merck in the pharmaceutical industry, Dupont Canada Inc., the financial consulting firm KPMG and the Royal Bank of Canada.

Trained as a research biochemist, Stephanie has written two books on biotechnology, Setting Genes to Work and The Biotechnology Revolution. She's been involved with and fascinated by the industry

for 20 years. "Once I saw that biotechnology would be able to pick apart the whole biological workings which I was familiar with, to me that was just a box of endless promise. It's never ceased to amaze me."

Although a scientific background is ideal for people interested in writing about biotechnology, Stephanie says it's not absolutely necessary.

Stephanie got her first taste of biotechnology in the late 70's when she worked for The New Scientist, one of the world's foremost science magazines, out of London, England, where she lived for 15 years. "We watched biotechnology grow out of the decade's various genetics research projects. At that time, I told the magazine that we had to follow this and get more involved. I started reporting on it and after a few months, I knew that I was hooked for life."

What skills do I need?

Although a scientific background is ideal for people interested in writing about biotechnology, Stephanie says it's not absolutely necessary. "I think it helps to have a science degree because you don't feel intimidated when you write about the area. But what you really need is passion. At The New Scientist, there were people who were not scientists, but they loved science and they brought a new dimension to it that we scientists didn't have. Because I was so turned on by the technology, sometimes I tended to get too involved with it, whereas they were able to stand back and get perspective."

"Be involved with other things. You'll be amazed at what you can bring to your science reporting."

A year after she joined The New Scientist, Stephanie won the Glaxo EEC Travelling Scholarship, Britain's foremost science writing prize. At the time, you didn't need a journalism degree. "I learned the needed skills at The New Scientist.". But things are different today. "Now, people are expected to have a journalism degree," she says.

According to Stephanie, to succeed as a science writer you need good writing skills, curiosity and a knack for communication. "You need an underlying desire to communicate that will give you endless patience when your editor wants to change things around."

She says your curiosity should extend beyond the boundaries of science. "Be involved with other things. You'll be amazed at what you can bring to your science reporting. The best reporters have that perspective and are informed about what else is going on in the world."

What is
the work like?

For journalists, "discipline is essential, especially if you're in business for yourself," explains Stephanie. "You'll find that time sometimes goes very quickly and you have nothing to show for it." Up at six, she gets her two kids ready for school before putting in an eight-hour work day. "This is a schedule I impose on myself. Without that kind of framework, you'll find it hard to earn a living", she adds.

Stephanie says that one of the most rewarding aspects of her work is when people say: That was a great story. You got me interested in something. "I can't imagine a bigger thrill." But journalism isn't all fun and games. "You have to be extremely accurate. In this kind of writing, you have to explain a lot of complicated theories very simply. You spend a lot of time thinking about it."

▶By Christine Daviault   (09/98)

TAKING CARE OF BUSINESS

Journalist
Administration and Regulation

■ What programme(s) I did:

B.Sc. in Biochemistry, McGill University, Quebec
M.Sc. in Information Science, London City University, U.K.
Diploma in Education, Bishops University, Quebec

■ Average salary

$60 000

■ What are other routes to this position?

Any scientific degree doubled by a journalism degree.

■ Skills and qualities you need for the job:

- need proven writing skills
- must have curiosity, eagerness to learn
- must have discipline, organisational skills
- should have a wide range of interests

"Information in Action"

When scientists have questions about the chemicals they're using or the experiments they're running, where do they go? To a library, of course. Scientists, who work at the Biotechnology Research Institute in Montreal, turn to **Eveline Landa**, head librarian for the Institute's Information Centre. Eveline uses the Internet, the World Wide Web, science databases as well as books and scientific journals to track down the facts researchers need.

What I do

Like any library, the Institute's Information Centre is packed with books and magazines. Eveline decides what goes on the Centre's shelves. To make her decisions, she consults catalogues sent to her by scientific publishing houses, reads magazine reviews or searches the Internet. Scientists also ask her to order certain books. "At first, when you don't have much experience as a librarian, you depend a lot on the users for suggestions," Eveline says. "But with experience, you learn more about what the users are looking for."

Eveline's favourite part of her job is helping scientists find information they need for their own research.

Eveline is also responsible for "weeding" or cleaning out the centre's collection each year to make room for new books. Deciding if a book has been used enough to make keeping it worthwhile is a tough decision, she says. But room is limited and some items must be thrown out.

Eveline's favourite part of her job is helping scientists find information they need for their own research. At the Institute, scientists research new drugs to treat diseases such as cancer, carry out experiments to clean contaminated land, air and water and help biotechnology companies run their laboratories better. Scientists might consult the library for information on how a particular chemical acts or how it is made or to find out about drugs or products made by other biotech companies

To answer those questions, Eveline turns to traditional places like books and encyclopaedias. She also logs onto her computer and searches several science databases or web sites run by universities or private companies.

What skills do I need?

Eveline decided to become a librarian after seeing an article encouraging people with a science background (she was finishing her B.Sc. in Biology) to apply for a Master's in Library Science. "At CEGEP, I loved working with my classmates at the library. I enjoyed finding books with the answers to questions the professors were asking." While working on her B.Sc., Eveline had a job as a university lab technician. She was often asked to go the library to look up an article or find some information. "I realised that I had some skill in this area," she says.

Today, people with a bachelor's degree in a scientific field (biology, chemistry, computer science or engineering) as well as a Master's in Library Science find work easily, Eveline says. Sometime, someone who has an M.Sc. or Ph.D. in Science but not a Library Science degree will be hired.

However, people thinking about becoming librarians should be sure they like working with people (in this case, mostly scientists) and they must have strong computer skills, including Internet use. "You don't have to love computer science, but you can't be afraid of technology." Librarians must also be proactive, she says. "You want to be just a bit ahead of your users and hope that one day, they will use the information that you discovered."

Often, Eveline teaches library users about the Internet and science databases so they can find information themselves.

Great librarians, Eveline adds, never give up. Sometimes, the information a scientist needs is very hard to find. But a librarian keeps on looking. "You can't just throw up your hands if you don't find what you need the first time. You have to try again," she says.

What is the work like?

"The work is very, very diverse," Eveline says. When she arrives at her office, at 8:30 a.m. each morning, she checks her email and telephone for information requests and spends an hour or two finding answers to these.

After that, she leaves her office to help scientists who come to the library. Often, Eveline teaches library users about the Internet and science databases so they can find information themselves. "We try to make people as autonomous as possible," she says.

Eveline doesn't travel very often for her job. She usually attends one large library science conference a year. But every few months, she'll attend workshops that teach librarians how to better use the science databases. However, Eveline says she doesn't need lots of travel outside the library to make her job interesting. "When someone gives us a complicated request, it becomes very exciting."

▶By Liz Warwick   (09/98)

Librarian

Administration and Regulation

■ What programme(s) I did:

M.A. in Library Science, University of Montreal, Quebec
B.Sc. in Biology, University of Montreal, Quebec

■ Average salary

$42 275

■ What are other routes to this position?

M.A. in Library Science combined with a B.Sc. in any science.

■ Skills and qualities you need for this job:

- must have background in science (biology, biochemistry, chemistry, pharmacology)
- need computer skills
- must be tenacious and thorough
- should like compiling and organising information

Photo : PPM, Montreal

"The Idea Police"

What are bacteria worth? Proteins? DNA sequences? In the biotechnology field, the figure might be in the millions of dollars. Bacteria, proteins and DNA can all be used to create products such as new drugs or medicines that can be very profitable for a company. To protect those profits, companies "patent" or protect their discoveries by turning for help to patent agents like **Andrew Bauer-Moore**.

What I do

A patent is a legal document granted by the Patent Office in Hull. "A patent gives an inventor the sole right to make, use and profit from an invention," Andrew says. It is given only to a new, groundbreaking and useful product, process or machine. The emphasis on "useful" means that vague things like an idea cannot be patented, Andrew says.

Patents are issued by individual countries which may vary in their definitions of what may and may not be patented. In Canada for example "higher-life forms" such as animals and humans may not be patented

while in the United States, a patent was issued for a mouse with altered genes.

To obtain a patent for an inventor, Andrew meets with him or her and discusses the invention. Through these talks, Andrew tries to write up the broadest and most complete description of the invention possible. "That's where the patent agent's art comes in," Andrew says. The agent is trying to protect the invention as much as possible so someone doesn't make a minor change in it and apply for a patent as well.

"Good writing and speaking skills are extremely important."

Once he has a complete, broad description, Andrew does research to find out if such a product, process or machine already exists. He looks through files at the Patent Office as well as checking specialised computer databases. If he thinks the invention is new and groundbreaking, he'll prepare a patent application and submit it to the Patent Office. From there, a person at the Patent Office called an "examiner" looks over the application, decides if the invention is new and useful and then either grants the patent or doesn't.

What skills
do I need?

"Getting hired as a patent agent trainee is a competitive process," Andrew says. "Good writing and speaking skills are extremely important." Agents need good listening skills, so they can understand what an inventor has created and why that invention is important enough to patent.

Becoming a patent agent is one of the few professions left where apprenticing or learning from more experienced patent agents is the norm. Andrew says agents usually have a Bachelor's degree in a science-related field and many have a law degree as well before they are hired as apprentices. The apprentices, or trainees, do all the work of a licensed patent agent except that their patent applications are reviewed by an agent before they are sent to the Patent Office.

Andrew came to the patent agent field with a Ph.D. in Chemistry. He'd worked as a researcher in several different countries including England and Israel. Then, having invented (with other people) and patented two products, he got interested in the patent process. He called up a large law firm specialising in intellectual property and asked them about how to become an agent. When they heard his background, the com-pany asked him in for an interview and offered him a job as a trainee.

After meeting many patent agents, Andrew says, "there is room for many different per-sonalities in this field." However, he adds, patent agents must be methodical and meticulous. If a patent isn't well written, and a competitor succeeds in patenting a similar product, a company can lose millions of dollars.

What is
the work like?

Andrew arrives at his office around 8:30 a.m. He sets his own agenda depending on what projects need to be finished. Some days, he'll go out and meet with an inven-tor. Other days, he'll do research at the Patent Office or use his computer to search various databases.

Andrew handles lots of paper during the day, from the patent applications them-selves to information obtained from his searches. However, he doesn't see the job as being about "paperwork." He often talks with his colleagues and asks them ques-tions. He also gets out and talks with the inventors. The stress level can be high, he admits, and he tends to work long hours. But Andrew doesn't regret it. "For me, this job is an ideal combination of my love of science and my love of language," he says.

▶By Liz Warwick   (09/98)

HEALTH

Patent Agent
Administration and Regulation

■ What programme(s) I did:

B.Sc. in Chemistry, McGill University, Quebec
Ph.D. in Bio-organic and Coordination Chemistry, McGill University, Quebec

■ Average salary

$50 500

■ What are other routes to this position?

A bachelor's degree in science, often with graduate degree and/or a law degree. One must pass the patent agent exam to become an agent.

■ Skills and qualities you need for this job:

- need excellent writing and speaking skills
- must be extremely methodical and meticulous
- must be well-organised
- must enjoy working under stress

"The Buying Game"

When **Bryan Singfield** goes to work every morning, he may just be helping to save the earth. Bryan works as a purchasing agent at Earth Alive, a small company that is developing a liquid organic biofertiliser which promises to be an effective and environmentally sound way to grow crops. "Humanity is destroying this planet. Agricultural biotech is focused on finding solutions. It's an exciting field because people in our business are financially successful and saving the environment at the same time," he says.

What I do

Earth Alive was founded in 1994, and is still conducting research on a liquid it produces - designed to carry bacteria and fungi which perform two useful jobs. The liquid acts as an environmentally-friendly pesticide and a solution to clean up oil spills. Earth Alive hopes to put its liquid on the market in the next year or two, and begin selling it in North America and Central America.

As purchasing agent, Bryan is responsible for handling incoming orders and deliveries of all the supplies and equipment Earth Alive needs in day-to-day operations. When Bryan joined Earth Alive two years ago, he had to find the basic materials the company needed to start up its work. He found a research facility/warehouse for the company, and compiled a list of parts and services that the company would need.

Today, Bryan is in charge of the company's 2000-square-foot testing facility in Waterloo, Quebec, where he handles all purchasing of supplies. His suppliers range from farm tool and implement suppliers who provide equipment for testing, to office equipment suppliers, Internet servers, and telephone and electricity companies. Bryan also finds independent laboratories to do some of the testing of Earth Alive's liquid, and chemical companies to provide the various ingredients needed to test Earth Alive's liquid on farms.

What skills do I need?

Bryan is a Certified General Accountant, and he frequently draws upon his accountancy training in his duties as a purchasing agent. "Being a purchasing agent is almost one and the same as accountancy work," he says. One important skill he picked up in accountancy school was how to set up inventory and accounts payable systems, which are essential to monitor a company's expenses and to make sure money isn't disappearing without being accounted for.

Purchasing agents also require good research skills. It is up to Bryan to find the best supplies at the best price, and this task can involve many phone calls.

According to Bryan, a good purchasing agent also needs a number of personal qualities. "You have to be friendly, you have to treat people with respect. You have to be patient, and you have to be committed to getting the job done." You also have to be persistent. "You're not always the number one client with the person on the other end of the phone."

Bryan is on call seven days a week, and works anywhere from 40 to 70 hours a week.

Students who want to follow in Bryan's footsteps should take a "well-rounded" approach to their business education. "Try to find summer jobs that will give you the opportunity to look at different areas of the operation of a business," he says, "like a shipping dock or a warehouse to get a feel for the flow of business and shipping, then in a store or office to learn about business cycles and dealing with customers."

What is
the work like?

Bryan is on call seven days a week, and works anywhere from 40 to 70 hours per week. But part of what explains this hectic schedule is the fact that he works for a small company. Working for a "start up" company, as new companies like his are called, usually means erratic hours; periods of intense activity followed by more relaxed periods. "You have to work when the work is there," explains Bryan. "And when you get on top of things, you can lay back a little bit. When the company has a lot of work, they don't want to see you punching out at five."

Bryan's job involves a lot of travelling. He says that purchasing agents should always be ready to pack their bags.

A purchasing agent who works for a larger company would work more regular hours, probably 7 to 3, five days per week. Bryan says that while his hours might be long, they are fulfilling. "If you're doing something you enjoy, it doesn't actually feel like you're getting up to go to work every morning. Not everybody finds that kind of satisfaction in their life, but when you do, it is pretty amazing."

Bryan's job involves a lot of travelling. He says that purchasing agents should always be ready to pack their bags. "This job can be very glamorous," he says. "You might have to travel to trade shows and supplier's plants. You're constantly on the lookout for better suppliers with better products, and you want to remain on the cutting edge."

▶By Wallie Seto and Sylvain Comeau (09/98)

ENVIRONMENT

Purchasing Agent
Administration and Regulation

■ What programme(s) I did:

Bachelor of Business Administration (B.BA), Bishop's University, Quebec
Certified General Accountancy, University of Calgary, Alberta

■ Average salary

$40 277

■ What are other routes to this position?

Students wanting to learn the job of a purchasing agent before going out into the workforce could go to technical schools, either CEGEPs in Quebec, or community colleges elsewhere in Canada.

■ Skills and qualities you need for this job:

- need good "people" skills
- need good negotiation skills
- must have strong research skills

"Trouble shooter"

Photo : Daniels & Gilonna Photography, Toronto

Judith Halmos-Stark likes to say that Wyeth-Ayerst Canada's vast range of products "covers everything from the womb to the tomb." In her role as Director of Regulatory Affairs, she oversees all regulatory aspects of the company's products. Wyeth-Ayerst, a research-oriented firm present in 145 countries and based in Philadelphia, Pennsylvania, USA, employs more than 40 000 people world-wide, including 1 600 in Canada.

What I do

As Director of Regulatory Affairs, Judith sees her job as a series of interlocking tasks. First, she must know the regulatory requirements for all of Wyeth-Ayerst's products, including women's contraceptives, cardiovascular and metabolic disease therapies, anti-inflammatory agents, central nervous system drugs, vaccines, infant formulas and more. Then she has to get these products registered, which means receiving government permission to sell them. Once the drug is approved and is marketed, Judith and her department have to make sure it remains in compliance with regulations. "Any changes have to be reviewed by regulatory affairs to see if they fit the original approval from the government, or if another submission will be required," explains Judith.

The Regulatory Affairs department's role is to insure Wyeth-Ayerst's products comply with the Canadian Food and Drug Act, enacted to protect the Canadian public. For every product, "you have to prove efficacy, safety and quality," says Judith. For example, to sell a new vaccine, the company must prove with scientific evidence that a drug is completely safe and stipulate its possible side effects. Such evidence can include toxicology reports, clinical trial test results and other data pertaining to governmental concerns.

As Director, Judith develops overall strategies for the regulatory affairs department, as well as insuring its efficiency and effectiveness. When the company has a new product, she meets with her team to draw up approval guidelines, and to make sure they have thought of all aspects of a submission. In addition to preparing and filing submissions, Judith answers questions and provides advice about regulatory matters to other departments at Wyeth-Ayerst. They might, for example, ask her opinion about the type of scientific information needed for government approval.

"Experience is key, because regulations and regulatory practices are not really taught but acquired through experience."

Sometimes Judith also has to step in when problems come up between regulatory affairs and other departments. The marketing department, for example, might produce promotional material that doesn't comply with the government's original approval. In other words, the company can't advertise a product use that is not approved by the government. Judith might be called upon to find a compromise if both departments can't reach a solution within the confines of the approval.

What skills
do I need?

Judith, who holds an Honours B.Sc. in Biochemistry, believes a science background is essential in order to understand the complex process and scientific data integral to regulatory affairs. "At the same time, experience is key, because regulations and regulatory practices are not really taught but acquired through experience," she says.

Besides these obvious requirements, Judith says good communication and interpersonal skills are necessary. "It's difficult to tell someone something doesn't comply." She believes it's regulatory affairs people's job to be creative in the way they deal with problems, which means presenting data in original ways that are still in regulatory compliance.

Judith, who completed a Medical Writing certificate, also stresses the importance of good writing skills. "A big part of regulatory

affairs is being able to present complex data in a very clear and concise fashion because, after all, the only thing the people in Ottawa have is the written documents. If you're not presenting that information clearly, you're going to lengthen the review process as they get back to you for clarifications. So you really have to be detail-oriented and meticulous in your writing."

What is
the work like?

Judith works in a closed office on the ninth floor of a modern office building in North York, where Wyeth-Ayerst has its head office. "Most regulatory affairs people have a closed office because they deal with sensitive information," she says. Her desk, bathed in sunlight provided by large bay windows, is equipped with a computer, an essential tool for her work.

Judith's job requires her to travel fairly often, since her staff is divided between Montreal and Toronto. She says she is on the road once every second week. Her tasks vary greatly depending on where she is. "When in Ottawa, I meet with the government. In Montreal, I deal with issues stemming from the activities of my group there, as well as any issues coming up from the manufacturing plant."

▶By Christine Daviault   (09/98)

HEALTH

Regulatory Affairs Director
Administration and Regulation

■ What programme(s) I did:

Honours B.Sc. in Biochemistry, Concordia University, Quebec
Certificate in Medical Writing through the American Medical Writers Association

■ Average salary

$90 322

■ What are other routes to this position?

Any science degree with good writing skills.

■ Skills and qualities you need for this job:

- must be detail-oriented
- need good writing and communication skills
- need good interpersonal skills

"Passing the Test"

AgrEvo Canada is an agricultural biotech company which produces plants "designed" with certain characteristics such as resistance to herbicides, insects, and disease. But the challenge in producing such plants is not only scientific. All these plants must pass the many safety and utility tests national governments set out to protect consumers, a process which requires a constant exchange of information between the company and the governments. As the director of regulatory affairs at AgrEvo, **Margaret Gadsby** co-ordinates the staff handling that information, and makes sure AgrEvo's products are approved for sale.

What I do

AgrEvo has 8500 employees and operates in more than 70 countries. Margaret heads the department of regulatory affairs in North America, supervising staff in Ottawa, the United States and Mexico. Regulatory affairs provides the information necessary to prove their products' safety and usefulness. Biotechnology products must be proven safe for the environment and consumers (human or animal) before governments grant companies approval to sell them.

Margaret co-ordinates the staff who compile data packages containing answers to extensive questions set by governments on things like plants' genetic makeup and nutritional value and toxicity. Separate reports are also filed to answer questions regarding food safety and environmental concerns. A single report can be as long as 5 000 pages while a package sent to the government can be a metre high!

Each government has different regulatory procedures, so one answer doesn't fit all. The challenge for Margaret's staff is to answer all their concerns adequately, by providing clear, comprehensible information. "We act as an interpreter between the company and government," she says.

After fifteen years in regulatory affairs, Margaret spends most of her time dealing with what she calls "big picture policy". This includes finding ways to help the government understand new products that don't fit the traditional categories, and dealing with changes in how governments perceive products. This sort of work might be necessary for new kinds of products, safety tests or situations like combining multiple genes for the first time.

What skills
do I need?

Margaret believes a background in biology and chemistry, doubled with applied research experience, is necessary to succeed in her field. "Techniques may change but not the foundations of life. If you have a really solid grounding in biology and chemistry, I think you're well on your way."

Her own scientific background is in entomology – the study of insects. She graduated with a B.Sc. Honours in that field with a minor in freshwater ecology, backed by training in statistics and computers. She also holds a master's in biological insect control.

While a science background is essential to her job, Margaret says so-called "soft skills" are also key. "To deal with governments what you need most are communication skills including the ability to listen, as well as patience and perseverance, because a lot of things move very slowly. You have to be able to endure that," she says.

Margaret's job is not for the weak.

"You also have to be able to read people reasonably well," she adds. "In order to be a good negotiator, to read between the lines, you need empathy. You must be able to put yourself in the shoes of the people across the table and understand what they're trying to accomplish. If you're going to suggest win-win situations, you have to understand what they're aiming for. You have to respect them."

What is
the work like?

Margaret's job is not for the weak. Because she is in constant contact with the rest of the world, she lives at the mercy of time zones, making phone calls to Europe in the morning and Japan at night, from her home. A lot of her work is done through email because of time differences.

Margaret works long hours, and spends a almost a third of the year travelling . When she's in the office, she admits to cutting herself a little slack. "I'm not a morning person so I don't generally come in really early but I'm usually here at least 45 minutes after closing," she says.

While wonderful, the travelling can also be gruelling. "I give up a lot of weekends to be en route to somewhere. I also work a lot of weekends because things pile up while I'm gone. A lot of people think life on the road is a perk, that it's exciting and you get to go to museums. I tend to work from 6 a.m. until midnight." Margaret says that after long travels, she often comes back with a cold!

▶By Christine Daviault   (09/98)

AGRICULTURE

Regulatory Affairs Specialist
Administration and Regulation

■ What programme(s) I did:

B.Sc. in Entomology, McMaster University in Hamilton, Ontario
M.Sc. in Entomology, University of British Columbia, British Columbia

■ Average salary

$62 195

■ What are other routes to this position?

At least one science discipline, plus people skills.

■ Skills and qualities you need for this job:

- need managerial skills
- must have strong negotiating skills
- need presentation skills

Photo : PPM, Montreal

"Reducing Risks"

Catherine Italiano lives and works in the city, but her job focuses on farms. As a toxicologist, she studies "livestock feed"; the food given to farm animals. Her job is to make sure the food is safe for animals, for any humans who eat meat, milk or eggs from those animals and for the environment.

What I do

Catherine works for the Canadian Food Inspection Agency, the government agency that ensures the safety of human and animal foods. Catherine works in the animal feeds section and often deals with biotechnology issues.

Many companies want to use biotechnology products such as genetically-altered plants to make animal feeds. For example, cooking oil is made from canola seeds. The residue makes a nutritious food for animals. However, canola farmers have recently begun to plant genetically-altered, herbicide-resistant seeds. These increase farm productivity since the genetically-altered plants are more resistant to powerful chemicals used to destroy weeds.

However, plants grown from altered seeds aren't always suitable for animal consumption. "People used to think that if something was approved for human use, it was OK for animals," she says. "That's a false assumption. We humans may eat an additive or a food colouring only once in a while. But animals eat the same food day after day. Therefore, the potential for harm is greater."

Before genetically-altered plants such as canola are fed to animals, feed companies must get Catherine's approval. The company sends her a detailed report on how and why the plant has been changed.

Catherine looks carefully at all the information and writes up a report called a risk assessment. She makes use of her studies in molecular biology and ecotoxicology and consults other experts at the Agency, then writes a report stating whether the new canola plant is as nutritious as the old one, or whether it could harm animals eating it in any way.

If Catherine says the product is safe, then the company can use it. If she thinks it's not safe, then the company either has to find another product or give her more information to help her change her mind.

What skills
do I need?

"You can't learn to do a biotechnology risk assessment at school," Catherine says. The biotechnology field is too new and the job requires many different kinds of skills that don't fit neatly into one particular academic programme.

Catherine arrived at this job through biology. She had done a B.Sc. in Molecular Biology because she loved studying living things. She started working as a research assistant at a lab when she heard about a program in ecotoxicology where people studied how chemicals and other products affect the environment. She enrolled in the programme and eventually got a diploma in ecotoxicology.

When she heard about the job at the Agency, she applied and was hired. "I've been here six and a half years and have never been bored," she says. At the Agency, Catherine works with a team of people concerned with food safety. She often talks about new products with biologists, toxicologists, plant breeders and nutritionists. "It takes a lot of communication and openness to work with people from diverse backgrounds," she says.

Good public-speaking skills are also important, she adds. Canada's Food Inspection Agency is considered one of the best in the world and other countries turn to the agency for advice on ensuring safe foods for people and animals. Catherine often meets with people from different countries to talk about her work. "You need to be able to go out there and explain what you're doing and sell the programme," she says.

What is
the work like?

Catherine arrives at her office around 8:30 a.m. "Usually, there's already a line of people waiting outside my cubicle to talk to me," she says with a laugh. Because her work depends on input from many different people, Catherine rarely has long periods of time when she's alone. Meetings and discussions with colleagues are a big part of her job. Catherine often works late and she also brings home reports and scientific journals to read over the weekends.

For Catherine, the job of evaluating new products goes beyond issues of safety. Through her work, she's been able to create guidelines and make policies that protect Canadians. "I feel like I've made a difference for this country," she says.

▶By Liz Warwick   (09/98)

AGRICULTURE

Toxicologist
Administration and Regulation

■ What programme(s) I did:

B.Sc. in Molecular Developmental Biology, McGill University, Quebec
Diploma in Ecotoxicology, Concordia University, Quebec

■ Average salary

$58 000

■ What are other routes to this position?

People can come to this job from lots of different fields: biology, chemistry, or even biotechnology but need some background in molecular science. As for toxicology, several universities offer toxicology programmes including UQAM, University of Montreal and McGill University.

■ Skills and qualities you need for this job:

- need a background in molecular science
- must have strong analytical skills
- must be detail-oriented
- should have concern for the environment and public safety

131

"A Nobel Ambition"
Michael Smith

► By Janice Paskey

Photo : Courtesy of U. of British Columbia Biotechnology Laboratory

You need more than talent to become a Nobel Prize winning scientist. Determination, hard work and even a dose of good luck all go into the formula for success. As Michael Smith's story shows, geniuses are made, not born.

In 1993 **Michael Smith** heard the news that most only dream of. He had won a Nobel Prize for developing a new technique which made genetic research much easier. Working with a team of researchers at the Biotechnology Centre at the University of British Columbia, Smith, a chemist, had invented "site-directed mutagenesis" — a technique which allows scientists to make a genetic mutation at any precise spot on the DNA molecule.

DNA, or deoxyribonucleic acid, is the basic material in a cell that holds all the body's genetic material and transmits hereditary traits. Scientists know that making changes to the DNA — or mutating it — can change an organism (a form of plant or animal life). Genetically altering plants can make for hardier fruits and vegetables. In humans it means possibly doing away with scourges such as hereditary cancers. Until Smith's discovery, gene mutation was a tedious procedure which involved treating living cells or organisms with chemicals or radiation to observe what types of mutations resulted.

"Site-directed mutagensis" means that scientists can chemically produce a mutation and insert it exactly where they want it in the DNA molecule. This DNA is then put into a living thing where it copies itself and where the effect on the organism can be observed. Scientists the world over are finding genetic research easier and more precise because of this technology. Smith's discovery meant scientists could do their work faster and achieve swifter results.

"I was lucky on more than one occasion. You have to recognise your luck and then maybe change direction to take advantage of it."

Michael Smith's discovery didn't come because of genius alone. "You've got to really love doing research," he says. " It's got to be the thing you want to do because if you're doing pioneering research, you have to work hard. Things go wrong quite a lot. You've got to have a commitment to it." As part of the commitment, the 66-year-old Smith mentions working six days a week, 50 to 60 hours a week, including spending long hours in the lab doing experiments, reading scientific articles and supervising graduate students.

Smith says there was also an element of luck to it. "I was lucky on more than one occasion. You have to recognise your luck and then maybe change direction to take advantage of it."

Although he is a star scientist now, Michael Smith heard "no" plenty of times throughout his career.

Michael Smith came from a modest family in Blackpool, England. Both his parents had worked since they were teens and his father supported the family as a market gardener. Normally, there would have been no fancy schools for the Smith kids. But in his early exams, Michael Smith showed promise and won a scholarship to a private school. He was nervous about attending because none of his friends would be there, but his mother pushed him to go.

It wasn't easy and he didn't like it much, but Smith did well and went on to study chemistry at the University of Manchester. For his undergraduate degree, the future Nobel Prize winner ended up with a B average, even though he had carried an A throughout. He'd done poorly on the final set of exams. Smith says his "pride was wounded." However, he went on to obtain a doctoral degree, the advanced schooling necessary for an aspiring scientist, at the same university.

Although he is a star scientist now, Michael Smith heard "no" plenty of times throughout his career. After completing his doctorate, Smith applied to all the universities on the West Coast of the United States to do more advanced study and research, known as a post-doctoral fellowship. He was rejected everywhere. But once again, Smith ran into a bit of luck and seized an opportunity that would change his life. One of his friends from the University of Manchester had been offered fellowships at both the University of British Columbia and at Columbus, Ohio, and had opted for Ohio.

"So why don't you apply at UBC?" he asked.

Smith did, and was accepted. He couldn't have made a better move. Smith's adviser there was Har Gobind Khorana, a scientist who won a Nobel Prize himself in 1968 and became Smith's mentor, a person he could look up to for education and guidance. Smith's mentor got him interested in DNA, a change in direction which would ultimately head him towards a Nobel Prize.

But it wasn't smooth sailing from there, even when Smith had developed his revolutionary technique for studying DNA. The article Smith wrote on his technique, which he had submitted to one of the most prestigious molecular science publications, was rejected! "I was annoyed," said Smith. But he decided to rewrite the piece and submit it to another prestigious journal, the Journal of Biological Chemistry. There it caught the attention of many people.

After winning the Nobel Prize, Smith decided to shut down his lab. He wanted to leave the limited government funds available for scientific research to the next generation of scientists. The future of research "depends on whether the government wakes up to the fact that biomedical science needs better funding, otherwise we'll lose the best brains to the United States, and we've already lost too many people," he says.

Even though Smith has retired from actual research, he says he works about twice as hard as before! He is setting up a genome sequencing project for the B.C. Cancer Institute, and travels widely to speak on science and global issues. He wants the future to be bright for young scientists. "It's important to be flexible," he says, "and to change direction when an opportunity presents itself." Smith never let his disappointments discourage him, and he has a Nobel Prize to prove it. ∎

Training

Biotech Training Programmes

The following is a list of Canadian colleges and undergraduate universities offering courses related to biotechnology.

The institutions are grouped together according to level (college or university), and are listed by province in alphabetical order. Within each province, institutions are listed alphabetically, and following each institution is a list of courses (also in alphabetical order).

UNIVERSITIES

■ ALBERTA:

Athabasca University
P.O. Box 10 000
Athabasca, AB T9S 1A1
Tel: (403) 675-6168
Fax: (403) 675-6477
http://www.athabascau.ca

• B.Sc. Human Sciences

Augustana University College
4901 46th Avenue
Camrose, AB T4V 2R3
Tel: (800) 661-8714 or (403) 679-1132
Fax: (403) 679-1129
http://www.augustana.ab.ca

• B.Sc. Chemistry
• B.Sc. Biology

The King's University College
9125 50th Street NW
Edmonton, AB T6B 2H3
Tel: (403) 465-3500
Fax: (403) 465-3534
http://www.kingsu.ab.ca

• B.Sc. Biology & Chemistry
• B.Sc. Environmental Studies

University of Alberta
1A University Campus NW
Edmonton, AB T6G 2E1
Tel: (403) 492-3111
Fax: (403) 492-7172
http://www.ualberta.ca

• B.Sc. Biochemistry
• B.Sc. Cell Biology

• B.Sc. Chemistry
• B.Sc. Biological Sciences
  - Cell Biotechnology
  - Physiology & Developmental Biology
  - Invertebrate Biology
  - Microbiology
  - Molecular Genetics
  - Plant Biology

University of Calgary
2500 University Drive NW
Calgary, AB T2N 1N4
Tel: (403) 220-5110
Fax: (403) 282-7298
http://wwww.ucalgary.ca

• B.Sc. Biochemistry
• B.Sc. Biological Sciences
• B.Sc. Cellular, Molecular & Microbial Biology
• B.Sc. Chemistry

University of Lethbridge
4401 University Drive
Lethbridge, AB T1K 3M4
Tel: (403) 320-5700
Fax: (403) 329-2097
http://www.uleth.ca

• B.Sc. Agricultural Biotechnology
• B.Sc. Biochemistry
• B.Sc. Biological Sciences
• B.Sc. Chemistry

British Columbia Open Learning Agency - Open University
4355 Mathissi Place
Burnaby, BC V5G 4S8
Tel: (604) 431-3300
Fax: (604) 431-3333
http://www.ola.bc.ca

• B.Sc. Science

Royal Roads University
2005 Sooke Road
Victoria, BC V9B 5Y2
Tel: (250) 391-2511
Fax: (250) 391-2500
http://www.royalroads.ca

• B.Sc. Environmental Science

Simon Fraser University
8888 University Drive
Burnaby, BC V5A 1S6
Tel: (604) 291-3111
Fax: (604) 291-4969
http://www.sfu.ca

• B.Sc. Biochemistry
• B.Sc. Biological Sciences
• B.Sc. Chemistry
• B.Sc. Environmental Sciences
  - Biology
  - Chemistry

Trinity Western University
7600 Glover Road
Langley, BC V2Y 1Y1
Tel: (604) 888-7511
Fax: (604) 513-2061
http://www.twu.ca

• B.Sc. Biology
• B.Sc. Chemistry

University College of the Cariboo
P.O. Box 3010
Kamloops, BC V2C 6N3
Tel: (250) 828-5000
Fax: (250) 828-5086
http://www.cariboo.bc.ca

• B.Sc. Animal Biology
• B.Sc. General Biology
• B.Sc. Ecology & Environmental Biology
• B.Sc. Chemistry
• B.Sc. Environmental Chemistry

University of British Columbia
2329 West Mall
Vancouver, BC V6T 1Z4
Tel: (604) 822-4636
http://www.ubc.ca

• B.Sc. Biochemistry
  - Option A: Metabolic & Structural Aspects
  - Option B: Molecular Biology
• B.Sc. Biochemistry & Chemistry
• B.Sc. Biology & Chemistry
• B.Sc. Cell & Developmental Biology
• B.Sc. General Biology
• B.Sc. Chemistry
• B.Sc. Microbiology
  - Option A: Molecular Microbiology & Biotechnology
  - Option B: Environmental Microbiology
  - Option C: Immunology
• B.Sc. Pharmacology

University of Northern British Columbia
3333 University Way
Prince George, BC V2N 4Z9
Tel: (250) 960-5555
Fax: (250) 960-6330
http://www.unbc.edu

• B.Sc. Biology

University of Victoria
P.O. Box 1700
Victoria, BC V8W 2Y2
Tel: (250) 721-7211
Fax: (250) 721-8653
http://www.uvic.ca

• B.Sc. Biology
• B.Sc. Chemistry
• B.Sc. Biochemistry & Microbiology

Kwantlen University College
12666 77th Avenue
Surrey, BC V3W 2M8
Tel: (604) 599-2100
Fax: (604) 599-2068
http://gateway.kwantlen.bc.ca

Environmental Protection Technology Diploma

Malaspina University College
900 Fifth Street
Nanaimo, BC V9R 5S5
Tel: (250) 753-3245
Fax: (250) 755-8725
http://www.mala.bc.ca

• B.Sc. Biology
• B.Sc. Fisheries & Aquaculture
Fisheries & Aquaculture Technology
Diploma

Okanagan University College
1000 KLO Road.
Kelowna, BC V1Y 4X8
Tel: (250) 762-5445
Fax: (250) 862-5466
http://www.ouc.bc.ca

• B.Sc. General Biology
• B.Sc. General Chemistry
• B.Sc. Environmental Chemistry
• B.Sc. Freshwater Science

University College of the Fraser Valley
33844 King Road
Abbotsford, BC V2S 7M9
Tel: (604) 853-7444
Fax: (604) 855-7614
http://www.ucfv.bc.ca

• B.Sc. Biology
• B.Sc. Double Minor Biology & Chemistry

■ MANITOBA:

Brandon University
270 18th Street
Brandon, MB R7A 6A9
Tel: (204) 728-9520
Fax: (204) 726-4573
http://www.brandonu.ca

• B.Sc. Botany
• B.Sc. Chemistry

University of Manitoba
66 Chancellors Circle
Winnipeg, MB R3T 2N2
Tel: (204) 474-8880
Fax: (204) 269-6629
http://www.umanitoba.ca

• B.Sc. Botany
• B.Sc. Chemistry
• B.Sc. Genetics
• B.Sc. Microbiology
• B.Sc. Biochemistry.
• B.Sc. Biotechnology
• B.Sc. Zoology

University of Winnipeg
515 Portage Avenue
Winnipeg, MB R3B 2E9
Tel: (204) 786-7811
Fax: (204) 786-8656
http://www.uwinnipeg.ca

• B.Sc. Biology
• B.Sc. Biology/Biological
  Technology Diploma
• B.Sc. Chemistry
• B.Sc. Applied Chemistry
• B.Sc. Molecular Biology

**Collège Universitaire de
Saint-Boniface**
200, Avenue de la Cathédrale
Saint-Boniface, MB R2H 0H7
Tel: (204) 233-0210
Fax: (204) 237-3240
http://www.ustboniface.mb.ca

• B.Sc. Biochemistry & Microbiology

■ NEW BRUNSWICK:

Mount Allison University
Sackville, NB E4L 1E4
Tel: (506) 364-2269
Fax: (506) 364-2272
http://www.mta.ca

• B.Sc. Biochemistry
• B.Sc. Chemistry
• B.Sc. Biology

University of New Brunswick
P.O. Box 4400
Fredericton, NB E3B 5A3
Tel: (506) 453-4666
Fax: (506) 453-4599
http://www.unb.ca

• B.Sc. Biology
• B.Sc. Chemistry

University of Moncton
Moncton, NB E1A 3E9
Tel: (506) 858-4000
Fax: (506) 585-4544
http://www.umoncton.ca

• B.Sc. Biochemistry
• B.Sc. Biology
• B.Sc. Chemistry

Memorial University of Newfoundland
P.O. Box 4200
St. John's, NF A1C 5S7
Tel: (709) 737-8000
Fax: (709) 737-4569
http://www.mun.ca

- B.Sc. Biochemistry
- B.Sc. Biology
- B.Sc. Cell Biology/Microbiology
- B.Sc. Chemistry
- Aquaculture Advanced Diploma
  (Fisheries & Marine Institute)
- Food Technology Advanced Diploma
  (Fisheries & Marine Institute)

■ NOVA SCOTIA:

Acadia University
Wolfville, NS B0P 1X0
Tel: (902) 542-2201 or 585-2201
Fax: (902) 585-1081
http://www.acadiau.ca

- B.Sc. Biology

Dalhousie University
Halifax, NS B3H 3J5
Tel: (902) 494-2211
Fax: (902) 494-2319
http://www.dal.ca

- B.Sc. Biochemistry (Minor in Chemistry)
- B.Sc. Chemistry (Minor in Biochemistry)
- B.Sc. Biology (Minor in Biochemistry)
- B.Sc. Marine Biology
- B.Sc. Microbiology & Biochemistry

Mount Saint Vincent University
Halifax, NS B3M 2J6
Tel: (902) 457-6128
Fax: (902) 457-6498
http://www.msvu.ca

- B.Sc. Biology
- B.Sc. Chemistry

Saint Mary's University
923 Robie Street
Halifax, NS B3H 3C3
Tel: (902) 420-5400
Fax: (902) 420-5151
http://www.stmarys.ca

- B.Sc. Biology
- B.Sc. Chemistry

St. Francis Xavier University
P.O. Box 5000
Antigonish, NS B2G 2W5
Tel: (902) 863-3300
Fax: (902) 867-5458
http://www.stfx.ca

- B.Sc. Biology
- B.Sc. Chemistry

University College of Cape Breton
P.O. Box 5300
Sydney, NS B1P 6L2
Tel: (888) 959-9995 or (902) 539-5300
Fax: (902) 562-0119
http://www.uccb.ns.ca

- B.Sc. Biology
- B.Sc. Chemistry

University of King's College
6350 Coburg Road
Halifax, NS B3H 2A1
Tel: (902) 422-1271
Fax: (902) 423-3357
http://www.ukings.ns.ca

See Dalhousie University for list
of programmes.

Université Sainte-Anne
Pointe-de-l'Eglise, NS B0W 1M0
Tel: (902) 769-2114
Fax: (902) 769-2930
http://ustanne-59.ustanne.ednet.ns.ca

- B.Sc. Biology (First two years only)
- B.Sc. Chemistry (First two years only)

Nova Scotia Agricultural College
P.O. Box 550
Truro, NS B2N 5E3
Tel: (902) 893-6600
Fax: (902) 895-5529
http://www.nsac.ns.ca

- B.Sc. Agricultural Chemistry
- B.Sc. Aquaculture
- B.Sc. Environmental Biology
- B.Sc. Plant Sciences
- Biology Technology Diploma
- Chemistry Laboratory
  Technology Diploma
- Food Quality Technology Diploma

Brock University
500 Glenridge Avenue
St. Catharines, ON L2S 3A1
Tel: (905) 688-5550
Fax: (905) 988-5488
http://www.brocku.ca

• B.Sc. Biotechnology
• B.Sc. Biochemistry
• B.Sc. Biology & Chemistry
• B.Sc. Chemistry

Carleton University
1125 Colonel By Drive
Ottawa, ON K1S 5B6
Tel: (888) 354-4414 or (613) 520-7400
Fax: (613) 520-3517
http://www.carleton.ca

• B.Sc. Biochemistry
• B.Sc. Biochemistry & Biotechnology
• B.Sc. Biology
• B.Sc. Biology & Biotechnology
• B.Sc. Chemistry

Lakehead University
955 Oliver Road
Thunder Bay, ON P7B 5E1
Tel: (807) 343-8110
Fax: (807) 343-8023
http://www.lakeheadu.ca

• B.Sc. Biology
• B.Sc. Chemistry

Laurentian University of Sudbury
935 Ramsey Lake Rd
Sudbury, ON P3E 2C6
Tel: (705) 675-1151
Fax: (705) 675-4891
http://www.laurentian.ca

• B.Sc. Biology
  - Biomedical Option
• B.Sc. Biochemistry
• B.Sc. Chemistry

McMaster University
1280 Main Street West
Hamilton, ON L8S 4L8
Tel: (905) 525-9140
Fax: (905) 527-0100
http://www.mcmaster.ca

• B.Sc. Biochemistry
  - Biochemistry Option
  - Molecular Biology, Biotechnology &
    Genetic Engineering Option

- Specialist Option
• B.Sc. Molecular Biology & Biotechnology
• B.Sc. Biochemistry & Chemistry
• B.Sc. Biological Chemistry
• B.Sc. Biology
• B.Sc. Biology & Pharmacology
• B.Sc. Chemistry

Nipissing University
P.O. Box 5002
North Bay, ON P1B 8L7
Tel: (705) 474-3450
Fax: (705) 474-1947
http://www.unipissing.ca

• B.Sc. General Science

Queen's University
Kingston, ON K7L 3N6
Tel: (613) 545-2000
Fax: (613) 545-2068
http://www.queensu.ca

• B.Sc. Biochemistry
• B.Sc. Biology
• B.Sc. Chemistry
• B.Sc. Life Sciences

Redeemer College
777 Garner Rd. E.
Ancaster, ON L9K 1J4
Tel: (905) 648-2131
Fax: (905) 648-2134
http://www.redeemer.on.ca

• B.Sc. Biology

Ryerson Polytechnic University
350 Victoria Street
Toronto, ON M5B 2K3
Tel: (416) 979-5000
Fax: (416) 979-5246
http://www.ryerson.ca

• B.Sc. Applied Chemistry & Biology

Trent University
1600 West Bank Dr.
Peterborough, ON K9J 7B8
Tel: (705) 748-1011
Fax: (705) 748-1629
http://www.trentu.ca

• B.Sc. Biochemistry
• B.Sc. Biology (Physiology & Medical
  Biology specialisation)
• B.Sc. Chemistry

University of Guelph

50 Stone Road East
Guelph, ON N1G 2W1
Tel: (519) 824-4120
Fax: (519) 766-9481
http://www.uoguelph.ca

- B.Sc. Animal Biology
- B.Sc. Bio-Medical Science
- B.Sc. Biochemistry
- B.Sc. Chemistry
- B.Sc. Microbiology
- B.Sc. Molecular Biology & Genetics
- B.Sc. Plant Biology
- B.Sc. Toxicology
- B.Sc. Toxicology
  - Environmental Toxicology Option
- B.Sc. Zoology

University of Ottawa

P.O. Box 450, Station A
Ottawa, ON K1N 6N5
Tel: (613) 562-5800
Fax: (613) 562-5105
http://www.uottawa.ca

- B.Sc. Biochemistry
- B.Sc. Biochemistry &
  Chemical Engineering
- B.Sc. Biology
  - Biotechnology Option
- B.Sc. Chemistry

University of Toronto

27 King's College Circle
Toronto, ON M5S 1A1
Tel: (416) 978-2011
Fax: (416) 978-2487
http://www.utoronto.ca

- B.Sc. Biochemistry
- B.Sc. Human Biology
- B.Sc. Immunology
- B.Sc. Microbiology
- B.Sc. Molecular Genetics &
  Molecular Biology
- B.Sc. Pharmacology
- B.Sc. Physiology
- B.Sc. Toxicology
- B.Sc. Biology
- B.Sc. Biological Chemistry
- B.Sc. Botany
- B.Sc. Molecular Plant Biology
- B.Sc. Chemistry

University of Waterloo

200 University Avenue West
Waterloo, ON N2L 3G1
Tel: (519) 885-1211
Fax: (519) 884-8009
http://www.uwaterloo.ca

- B.Sc. Biochemistry
- B.Sc. Biochemistry
  - Biotechnology Option
- B.Sc. Biology
- B.Sc. Biology & Chemistry
- B.Sc. Chemistry

University of Western Ontario

Stevenson-Lawson Building
London, ON N6A 5B8
Tel: (519) 679-2111
Fax: (519) 661-3388
http://www.uwo.ca

- B.Sc. Biochemistry
- B.Sc. Biochemistry & Chemistry
- B.Sc. Biology
- B.Sc. Biophysics
- B.Sc. Cell Biology
- B.Sc. Chemistry
- B.Sc. Genetics
- B.Sc. Microbiology & Immunology
- B.Sc. Pharmacology & Toxicology
- B.Sc. Plant Science

University of Windsor

401 Sunset Avenue
Windsor, ON N9B 3P4
Tel: (519) 253-4232
Fax: (519) 973-7050
http://www.uwindsor.ca

- B.Sc. Chemistry
- B.Sc. Biological Sciences
- B.Sc. Biochemistry

Wilfrid Laurier University

75 University Avenue West
Waterloo, ON N2L 3C5
Tel: (519) 884-1970
Fax: (519) 886-9351
http://www.wlu.ca

- B.Sc. Biology & Chemistry
- B.Sc. Chemistry

York University
4700 Keele Street
North York, ON M3J 1P3
Tel: (416) 736-2100
Fax: (416) 736-5444
http://www.yorku.ca

- B.Sc. Biology
- B.Sc. Chemistry & Biology
- B.Sc. Chemistry

■ PRINCE EDWARD ISLAND:

University of Prince Edward Island
550 University Avenue
Charlottetown, PE C1A 4P3
Tel: (902) 566-0300
Fax: (902) 566-0795
http://www.upei.ca

- B.Sc. Biology
- B.Sc. Chemistry

■ QUEBEC:

Bishop's University
Lennoxville, QC J1M 1Z7
Tel: (819) 822-9600
Fax: (819) 822-9661
http://www.ubishops.ca

- B.Sc. Biology
- B.Sc. Chemistry

Concordia University
1455, boulevard de Maisonneuve Ouest
Montréal, QC H3G 1M8
Tel: (514) 848-2424
Fax: (514) 848-2621
http://www.concordia.ca

- B.Sc. Chemistry
- B.Sc. Biochemistry
- B.Sc. Biochemistry & Molecular Biology
- B.Sc. Biology
- B.Sc. Cell & Molecular Biology

McGill University
845, rue Sherbrooke Ouest
Montréal, QC H3A 2T6
Tel: (514) 398-4455
Fax: (514) 398-3594
http://www.mcgill.ca

- B.Sc. Chemistry
- B.Sc. Biology
- Biotechnology
- Molecular Genetics & Development
- B.Sc. Biochemistry

Université de Montréal
C.P. 6128
Succursale Centre-Ville
Montreal, QC H3C 3J7
Tel: (514) 343-6111
Fax: (514) 343-2097
http://www.umontreal.ca

- B.Sc. Biochemistry
- B.Sc. Chemistry
- B.Sc. Biological Sciences
- Biological Sciences
- Microbiology & Immunology
- Biomedical Sciences
- Biology & Plant Biotechnology
- Animal Physiology

Université du Québec à Chicoutimi
555, boulevard de l'Université
Chicoutimi, QC G7H 2B1
Tel: (418) 656-5011
Fax: (418) 545-5012
http://www.uqac.uquebec.ca

- B.Sc. Biology
- B.Sc. Chemistry

Université du Québec à Montréal
C.P. 8888
Succursale Centre-Ville
Montréal, QC H3C 3P8
Tel: (514) 987-3000
Fax: (514) 987-8932
http://www.uqam.ca

- B.Sc. Chemistry
- B.Sc. Biochemistry
- Physiology & Toxicology
- Molecular Biology & Biotechnology

Université du Québec à Rimouski
C.P. 3300
300, allée des Ursulines
Rimouski, QC G5L 3A1
Tel: (418) 723-1986
Fax: (418) 724-1525
http://www.uqar.uquebec.ca

- B.Sc. Chemistry
- General Biology
- Biochemistry
- Biology & Chemistry

Université du Québec à Trois-Rivières
C. P. 500
3351, boulevard des Forges
Trois-Rivières, QC G9A 5H7
Tel: (819) 376-5012
Fax: (819) 376-5211
http://www.uqtr.uquebec.ca

- B.Sc. Biology
  - Molecular Biology & Biotechnology
- B.Sc. Biology
- B.Sc. Medical Biology
- B.Sc. Chemistry

Université de Sherbrooke
2500, boulevard de l'Université
Sherbrooke, QC J1K 2R1
Tel: (819) 821-7000
Fax: (819) 821-7966
http://www.usherb.ca

- B.Sc. Biochemistry
- B.Sc. Biology
- B.Sc. Chemistry

Université Laval
Québec, QC G1K 7P4
Tel: (418) 656-3333
Fax: (418) 656-2809
http://www.ulaval.ca

- B.Sc. Biochemistry
- B.Sc. Biology
- B.Sc. Chemistry
- B.Sc. Microbiology
- Genetic Engineering Certificate

■ SASKATCHEWAN:

University of Regina
3737 Wascana Parkway
Regina, SK S4S 0A2
Tel: (306) 585-4111
Fax: (306) 585-5203
http://www.uregina.ca

- B.Sc. Biochemistry
- B.Sc. Biology
- B.Sc. Biology & Biochemistry
- B.Sc. Chemistry

University of Saskatchewan
105 Administration Place
Saskatoon, SK S7N 5A2
Tel: (306) 966-4343
Fax: (306) 966-3730
http://www.usask.ca

- B.Sc. Agricultural Biology
- B.Sc. Animal Science
- B.Sc. Food Science

COLLEGES

■ ALBERTA:

Concordia University College of Alberta
7128 Ada Boulevard NW
Edmonton, AB T5B 4E4
Tel: (403) 479-8481
Fax: (403) 474-1933
http://www.concordia.ab.ca

- Biology

Fairview College
11235 99th Av.
Fairview, AB T0H 1L0
Tel: (888) 999-7882 or (403) 835-6600
Fax: (403) 835-6698
http://www.fairviewc.ab.ca

- Animal Health

Grande Prairie Regional College
10726 106th Avenue
Grande Prairie, AB T8V 4C4
Tel: (888) 539-4772 or (403) 539-2911
Fax: (403) 539-2888
http://www.gprc.ab.ca

- Microbiology
- Genetics
- Cell Biotechnology
- Botany
- Biochemistry
- Biology

Grant MacEwan Community College
P.O. Box 1796
Edmonton, AB T5J 2P2
Tel: (403) 497-5040
Fax: (403) 497-5001
http://www.gmcc.ab.ca

- Biochemistry
- Cell Biology
- Cell Biotechnology
- Developmental Biology
- Environmental Biology
- Invertebrate Biology
- Microbiology
- Molecular Genetics
- Physiology
- Plant Biology

Keyano College
8115 Franklin Avenue
Fort McMurray, AB T9H 2H7
Tel: (403) 791-4850
Fax: (403) 791-4841
http://www.keyanoc.ab.ca

• Biological Sciences

Lakeland College
5707 47th Avenue West
Vermilion, AB T9X 1K5
Tel: (800) 661-6490 or (403) 853-8420
Fax: (403) 853-2955
http://www.lakelandc.ab.ca

• Animal Health

Medicine Hat College
299 College Drive SE
Medicine Hat, AB T1A 3Y6
Tel: (403) 529-3819
Fax: (403) 504-3517
http://www.mhc.ab.ca

• Biochemistry
• Biological Sciences
• Botany
• Cellular, Molecular, Microbial Biology
• Medical Laboratory Science

Northern Alberta Institute of Technology
11762 106th Street NW
Edmonton, AB T5G 3H1
Tel: (403) 471-7400
Fax: (403) 471-8583
http://www.nait.ab.ca

• Animal Health
• Environmental Sciences
• Laboratory & Research
• Renewable Resources
• Chemical Technology
• Cytotechnology
• Medical Laboratory Technology

Olds College
4500 50th Street
Olds, AB T4H 1R6
Tel: (800) 661-6537 or (403) 556-8281
Fax: (403) 556-4711
http://www.oldscollege.ab.ca

• Animal Health

Red Deer College
P.O. Box 5005
56th Ave. & 32nd St.
Red Deer, AB T4N 5H5
Tel: (403) 342-3300
Fax: (403) 340-8940
http://www.rdc.ab.ca

• Chemical Technology

Southern Alberta Institute of Technology
1301 16th Avenue NW
Calgary, AB T2M 0L4
Tel: (403) 284-8110
Fax: (403) 284-8851
http://www.sait.ab.ca

• Animal Health
• Chemical Technology
• Food & Nutrition Management
• Medical Laboratory Assistant

■ *BRITISH COLUMBIA:*

British Columbia Institute of Technology
3700 Willingdon Avenue
Burnaby, BC V5G 3H2
Tel: (604) 434-5734
Fax: (604) 430-1331
http://www.bcit.bc.ca

• Biotechnology

Camosun College
3100 Foul Bay Road
Victoria, BC V8P 5J2
Tel: (250) 370-3000
Fax: (250) 370-3551
http://www.camosun.bc.ca

• Chemistry & Biochemistry
• Environmental Science
• Biology
• Chemistry

Capilano College
2055 Purcell Way
North Vancouver, BC V7J 3H5
Tel: (604) 986-1911
Fax: (604) 984-4985
http://www.capcollege.bc.ca

• Biology
• Chemistry
• Environmental Science
• Associate Degree in Science

College of New Caledonia
3330 22nd Avenue
Prince George, BC V2N 1P8
Tel: (250) 562-2131
Fax: (250) 561-5816
http://www.cnc.bc.ca

• Associate Degree in Science

College of the Rockies
P.O. Box 8500
2700 College Way
Cranbrook, BC V1C 5L7
Tel: (250) 489-2751
Fax: (250) 489-8253
http://www.cotr.bc.ca

• Associate of Science

Langara College
100 West 49th Avenue
Vancouver, BC V5Y 2Z6
Tel: (604) 323-5511
Fax: (604) 323-5555
http://www.langara.bc.ca

• Environmental Studies

Nicola Valley Institute of Technology
P.O. Box 399
Merritt, BC V0K 2B0
Tel: (250) 378-3300
Fax: (250) 378-3332

• Diploma of Technology

North Island College
2300 Ryan Road
Courtenay, BC V9N 8N6
Tel: (250) 334-5000
Fax: (250) 334-5018
http://www.nic.bc.ca

• Environmental Assessment
• Associate of Science

■ MANITOBA:

Red River Community College
2055 Notre Dame Avenue
Winnipeg, MB R3H 0J9
Tel: (204) 632-3960
Fax: (204) 632-9661
http://www.rrcc.mb.ca

• Chemical and Biosciences

■ NEW BRUNSWICK:

New Brunswick Community Colleges
Dept. of Advanced Education & Training
P.O. Box 6000
470 York St.
Fredericton, NB E3B 5H1
Tel: (506) 453-2597
Fax: (506) 453-3806
http://www.gov.nb.ca/ael/nbcc/

• Agricultural
• Biotechnology Co-Op
• Chemical Technician
• Environmental Technology
• Food Technology

■ NEWFOUNDLAND:

College of the North Atlantic
P.O. Box 5400
432 Massachusetts Drive
Stephenville, NF A2N 2Z6
Tel: (709) 643-7701
Fax: (709) 643-5407
http://www.northatlantic.nf.ca

• Biotechnology

■ ONTARIO:

Algonquin College
1385 Woodroffe Avenue
Nepean, ON K2G 1V8
Tel: (613) 727-4723
Fax: (613) 727-7767
http://www.algonquinc.on.ca

• Chemical Technology

Canadore College of Applied Arts and Technology
P.O. Box 5001
100 College Drive
North Bay, ON P1B 8K9
Tel: (705) 474-7600
Fax: (705) 474-2384
http://www.canadorec.on.ca

• Biotechnology

Centennial College
P.O. Box 631
Station A
Scarborough, ON M1K 5E9
Tel: (416) 289-5000
Fax: (416) 289-5106
http://www.cencol.on.ca

• Biological Technology

Durham College
2000 Simcoe Street North
Oshawa, ON LIH 7K4
Tel: (905) 721-2000
Fax: (905) 721-3113
http://www.durhamc.on.ca

• Environmental Technology
• Food and Drug Technology

Georgian College
I Georgian Drive
Barrie, ON L4M 3X9
Tel: (705) 728-1968
Fax: (705) 722-5123
http://www.georcoll.on.ca

• Environmental Engineering (Co-Op)

Humber College
205 Humber College Boulevard
Toronto, ON M9W 5L7
Tel: (416) 675-3111
Fax: (416) 675-2427
http://www.humberc.on.ca

• Chemical Engineering

La Cité Collégiale
801, promenade de l'Aviation
Ottawa, ON KIK 4R3
Tel: (613) 742-2483
Fax: (613) 742-2481
http://www.lacitec.on.ca

• Biotechnology

Lambton College
1457 London Road
Sarnia, ON N7S 6K4
Tel: (519) 542-7751
Fax: (519) 542-7982
http://www.lambton.on.ca

• Chemical Engineering
• Environmental Technology (Co-Op)

Loyalist College
P.O. Box 4200
Wallbridge-Loyalist Road
Belleville, ON K8N 5B9
Tel: (613) 969-1913
Fax: (613) 962-1376
http://www.loyalistc.on.ca

• Chemical Engineering
• Chemical Laboratory Assistant
• Environmental Technology

Michener Institute for Applied Health Sciences
222 St. Patrick Street
Toronto, ON M5T IV4
Tel: (800) 387-9066 or (416) 596-3101
Fax: (416) 596-3180
http://www.michener.on.ca

• Laboratory Sciences
• Genetics

Mohawk College
P.O. Box 2034
Hamilton, ON L8N 3T2
Tel: (905) 575-1212
Fax: (905) 575-2378
http://www.mohawkc.on.ca

• Chemical Engineering
• Chemical Technician
• Environmental Science

Northern College
P.O. Box 3211
Timmins, ON P4N 8R6
Tel: (800) 461-2167 or (705) 235-3211
Fax: (705) 235-7279
http://www.northernc.on.ca

• Environmental Studies
• Environmental Engineering
• Water Resources
• Veterinary Technician

Sault College
443 Northern Avenue
Sault Ste. Marie, ON P6A 5L3
Tel: (800) 461-2260 or (705) 759-6774
Fax: (705) 759-1319
http://www.saultc.on.ca

• Environmental Engineering
• Water Resources Engineering

Seneca College
1750 Finch Avenue East
North York, ON M2J 2X5
Tel: (416) 491-5050
Fax: (416) 491-3081
http://www.senecac.on.ca

• Biological Technician
• Biological Research
• Chemical Technology

Sheridan College
1430 Trafalgar Road
Oakville, ON L6H 2L1
Tel: (905) 845-9430
Fax: (905) 815-4043
http://www.sheridanc.on.ca

- Chemical Engineering
- Chemical Laboratory Technician
- Environmental Science

Sir Sandford Fleming College
Sutherland Campus
Brealey Drive
Peterborough, ON K9J 7B1
Tel: (705) 749-5530
Fax: (705) 749-5540
http://www.flemingc.on.ca

- Fish & Wildlife

St. Laurence College
2288 Parkedale Avenue
Brockville, ON K6V 5X3
Tel: (613) 345-0660
Fax: (613) 345-2231
http://www.stlaurencec.on.ca

- Animal Care
- Biotechnology
- Medical Laboratory Technology
- Veterinary Technology

■ PRINCE EDWARD ISLAND:

Holland College
140 Weymouth Street
Charlottetown, PE C1A 4Z1
Tel: (902) 566-9500
Fax: (902) 629-4239
http://www.hollandc.pe.ca

- Aquaculture
- Environmental Technology
- Renewable Resource Management

■ QUEBEC:

Collège Ahuntsic
9155, rue Saint-Hubert
Montréal, QC H2M 1Y8
Tel: (514) 389-5921
Fax: (514) 389-4554
http://www.collegeahuntsic.qc.ca

- Chemical Biology (Biotechnology)

Dawson College
3040, rue Sherbrooke Ouest
Westmount, QC H3Z 1A4
Tel: (514) 931-8731
Fax: (514) 931-3567
http://www.dawsoncollege.qc.ca

- Medical Laboratory Technology
- Chemical Technology

Vanier College
821, avenue Sainte-Croix
Saint-Laurent, QC H4L 3X9
Tel: (514) 744-7500
Fax: (514) 744-7520
http://www.vaniercollege.qc.ca

- Applied Ecology
- Animal Health

■ SASKATCHEWAN:

Saskatchewan Institute of Applied Science & Technology
P.O. Box 1520
Saskatoon, SK S7K 3R5
Tel: (306) 933-6350
Fax: (306) 933-6490
http://www.siast.sk.ca

- Biotechnology
- Chemical Technology

List of Biotech Resources

Organizations and Associations:

A list of national and regional bodies to supply you with the latest information on the biotech industry in Canada.

NATIONAL

Biotechnology Human Resource Council
420-130 Albert Street
Ottawa, ON K1P 5G4
Tel: (613) 235-1402
Fax: (613) 233-7541
http://www.bhrc.ca/

Food Biotechnology Communication Network
1 Stone Road West, 4th Floor
Guelph, ON N1G 4Y2
Tel: (519) 826-3440
Fax: (519) 826-3441
http://www.foodbiotech.org

BIOTECanada
420-130 Albert Street
Ottawa, ON K1P 5G4
Tel: (613) 230-5585
Fax: (613) 233-7541
http://www.biotech.ca/

The Biotechnology Network
301 Moodie Drive, Suite 205
Nepean, ON K2H 9C4
Tel: (613) 721-6658
Fax: (613) 721-6570

REGIONAL

• British Columbia:

British Columbia Biotechnology Alliance
3250 East Mall, Suite 220
Vancouver, BC V6T 1W5
Tel: (604) 221-3026
Fax: (604) 221-3027
http://www.biotech.bc.ca

• New Brunswick:

BioAtlantech
P.O. Box 636
Station A
Fredericton, NB E3B 5A6
Tel: (506) 444-2444
Fax: (506) 444-5662
http://www.bioatlantech.nb.ca

• Newfoundland:

Bio-East
Seabright Corporation Ltd.
Memorial University of Newfoundland
Spencer Hall
St. John's, NF A1C 5S7
Tel: (709) 737-2682
Fax: (709) 737-4029

• Nova Scotia:

BioNova
P.O. Box 790
101 Research Drive
Dartmouth, NS B2Y 3Z7
Tel: (902) 424-8670
Fax: (902) 424-4679

• Ontario:

Ontario Agri-Food Technologies
1 Stone Road West, 4th Floor
Guelph, ON N1G 4Y2
Tel: (519) 826-4195
Fax: (519) 826-3389
http://www.sentex.net/~oaft/

Ottawa Life Sciences Council
600 Peter Morand Crescent, Suite 100
Ottawa Life Sciences Technology Park
Ottawa, ON K1G 5Z3
Tel: (613) 521-4878
Fax: (613) 521-3065
http://www.olsc.ca/

Toronto Biotechnology Initiative
P.O. Box 446
Station A
Toronto, ON M5W 1C2
Tel: (416) 392-4780
Fax: (416) 397-0906
http://www.torontobiotech.org

• Prince Edward Island:

Enterprise PEI
P.O. Box 910
Charlottetown, PE C1A 7L9
Tel: (902) 368-5859
Fax: (902) 368-6301
http://www.gov.pe.ca/development/epei

• Quebec:

**Quebec Bio-Industries Association /
Association Québécoise des
bio-industries**
1555, boulevard Chomedey, Bureau 100
Laval, QC H7V 3Z1
Tel: (514) 978-5973
Fax: (514) 978-5970
http://www.aqb.qc.ca

• Saskatchewan:

Ag-West Biotech Inc.
101 111 Research Drive
Saskatoon, SK S7N 3R2
Tel: (306) 975-1939
Fax: (306) 975-1966
http://www.lights.com/agwest/

Internet Resources:

A list of Internet sites with general and career-related information on biotechnology, followed by some Internet sites to help you prepare for a successful career of your choice.

BIOTECH SITES

**Biotechnology Science Centre:
Industry Canada**
http://strategis.ic.gc.ca/learnbiotech
Educational resource that explains the science underpinning several leading-edge biotechnology applications.

**Biotechnology: Ethics and the Industry:
Industry Canada**
http://strategis.ic.gc.ca/biotechethics
Couples ethical consideration of scientific issues and industry initiative with legislation on national and international levels.

Biotechnology/Youth's Future
http://biotech.acadie.net
Magazine for Canadian youth.

Connaught Biotech Exhibition
http://www.ConnaughtBioExpo.com
Information on exhibits across Canada, articles, and links to other sites.

InfoBiotech Canada
http://www.ibc.nrc.ca/ibc
Comprehensive site by the National Research Council.

Access Excellence
http://www.gene.com/ae/
Biology teaching and learning resource.

149

Australian Biotechnology Association
http://www.aba.asn.au/leaflets.html
Introduction to basic industry concepts.

Biotech Resources (Indiana University)
http://biotech.chem.indiana.edu/pages/
scitools.html
Resource for scientists, educators and
students.

**National Biotechnology Information
Facility**
http://www.nbif.org
Comprehensive information site.

North Carolina Biotechnology Center
http://www.ncbiotech.org/aboutbt.htm
Introduction to concepts and terminology.

**University of Wisconsin Biotechnology
Education Program for the Public**
http://www.biotech.wisc.edu
Gateway to eduactional materials and
resources.

CAREER SITES

Careers in Canadian Biotech
http://www.biotecareers.com

**Career Development Manual—Career
Services University of Waterloo**
http://www.adm.uwaterloo.ca/infocecs/
CRC/manual-home.html

**Exploring Occupations: Getting You
Started on Your Career Path!
University of Manitoba.**
http://www.umanitoba.ca/student/
counselling/careers.html

MazeMaster
http://www.mazemaster.on.ca/

National Graduate Register
http://ngr.schoolnet.ca/home/
students.html

The Riley Guide
http://www.dbm.com/jobguide/

**What Color is Your Parachute: Job
Hunting Online**
http://www.washingtonpost.com/wp-
adv/classifieds/careerpost/parachute/
front.htm

WORKsearch
http://www.golden.net/~archeus/
worksrch.htm

WorkSearch (Government of Canada)
http://www.worksearch.gc.ca/

Monster Board Canada
http://www.monster.ca

Damn Good Resumes
http://www.damngood.com/
jobseekers/tips.html

Repertoire of Interviewees

This is a list of our interviewees, in alphabetical order according to job title. Their actual title at work follows, with the name of their company, address, phone and web site.

Clinical Research
Health

• Biotech Engineer 80

Bernard Boisvert
Manager, Engineering Department
Merck Frosst Canada Inc.
16711, route Transcanadienne
Kirkland, QC H9H 3L1
Tel: (514) 428-7920
Fax : (514) 428-4951
http://www.merckfrosst.ca
Manufacturing and Field Work
Health

• Business Development Analyst 82

Sylvie Masson
Business Development Analyst
Société Innovatech Grand Montréal
2020, rue Université, Suite 1527
Montreal, QC H3A 2A5
Tel:(514) 864-2929, 1-800-883-7319
Fax: (514) 864-4220
http://www.innovatech.qc.ca/
Sales and Marketing

• Business Development
  Manager 84

Deborah Bird
Business Development Manager
StemCell Technologies Inc.
808 777 West Broadway
Vancouver, BC V5Z 4J7
Tel: (604) 877-0713
Fax:(604) 877-0704
http://www.stemcell.com
Sales and Marketing
Health

• Business Programme
  Manager 104

Donna Viger
Manager of Business Programme and
Administrative Services
Institute for Marine Biosciences
1411 Oxford Street
Halifax, NS B3H 3Z1
Tel: 902-426-6829
Fax: 902-426-9413
http://www.nrc.ca/imb

Adminstration and Regulation
Aquaculture

• Chief Executive Officer 106

Dr. Francesco Bellini
Chief Executive Officer
BioChem Pharma Inc.
275, boulevard Armand-Frappier
Laval, QC H7V 4A7
Tel: (450) 978-7771
Fax: (450) 978-7755
http://biochem-pharma.com
Adminstration and Regulation
Health

• Chief Financial Officer 108

Dana Rath
Vice-President, Finance & Administration
Nexia Biotechnologies Inc.
21025, route Transcanadienne
Ste-Anne de Bellevue, QC H9X 3R2
Tel: (514)457-4522 ext.15
Fax: (514) 457-6151
html://www.nexiabiotech.com
Adminstration and Regulation
Health

• Clinical Research Associate 68

Paula Jones-Wright
Clinical Research Associate
Clinical Trials Atlantic Corp.
1484 Carlton Street
Halifax, NS B3H 3B7
Tel: (902) 494-6655
Fax: (902) 494-2057
http:\\www.ctac.org
Clinical Research
Health

• Communications Manager 110

Lisa Jategaonkar
Manager of Communications and Public
Awareness
Ag-West Biotech Inc.
101 111 Research Drive
Saskatoon, SK S7N 3R2
Tel: (306) 975-1939
Fax: (306) 975-1966
http://www.lights.com/agwest

Administration and Regulation
Agriculture

• Controller

Lucie St-Georges
Controller and V.P. Finance
BioSignal Inc.
1744, rue William, Suite 600
Montreal,QC H3J 1R4
Tel: (514) 937-1010
Fax: (514) 937-0777
http://www.biosignal.com
Administration and Regulation
Health

• Field Coordinator

Claudine Giguère
Field Coordinator
Algène Biotechnologies
8475, avenue Christophe-Colomb, Suite 1000
Montreal, QC H2M 2N9
Tel: (514) 850-2400
Fax: (514) 850-2424
info@algene.com
Clinical Research
Health

• Field Technician

Jason Chiasson
Project Technician
Geobac Technology Group Inc.
P.O. Box 3240
Station B
200 Prospect Street
Fredericton, NB E3A 5G9
Tel: (506) 451-1991
Fax: (506) 457-2100
geobacnb@nbnet.nb.ca
Manufacturing and Field Work
Environment

• Financial Analyst

Jean-Luc Berger
Financial Analyst
CrediFinance Securities Ltd.
130 Adelaide Street W., Suite 3303
Toronto, ON M5H 3P5
Tel: (416) 955-0159
Fax: (416) 364-1522
Sales and Marketing
Health

• Human Resources Manager

Catherine Sutter
Director of Human Resources
Kinetek Pharmaceuticals Inc.
1779 West 75th Avenue
Vancouver, BC V6P 6P2
Tel: (604) 269-2256
Fax: (604) 267-7667
csutter@kinetekpharma.com
Adminstration and Regulation
Health

• Industrial Adviser

Bill Dobson
Industrial Technology Adviser
Industrial Research Assistance Programme
(IRAP)
University of Toronto, Faculty of Medicine,
FitzGerald Building
150 College Street, Room 83B
Toronto, ON M5S 3E2
Tel: (416) 954-8330
Fax: (416) 954-8331
http://www.nrc.ca
Sales and Marketing

• Intellectual Property Manager

Dr. Leo Wong
Intellectual Property Manager
Cangene Corporation
26 Henlow Bay
Winnipeg, Manitoba R3Y 1G4
Tel: (204) 989-6709
Fax: (204) 487-4086
http://www.cangene.ca
Adminstration and Regulation
Health

• Investor Relations Manager

Jean Compton
Manager of Investor Relations
Cangene Corporation
3403 American Drive, Units 3/4
Mississuaga, ON L4V 1T4
Tel: (905) 673-0200
Fax: (905) 673-5123
http://www.cangene.ca
Sales and Marketing
Health

• Journalist

Stephanie Yanchinski
Science Journalist and Communications
Consultant
579 Glengrove Avenue W.
Toronto, ON M6B 2H5
Tel: (416) 781-4896
Fax: (416) 781-3030
Administration and Regulation
Health

• Lab Assistant

Julie Brais
Research Technician
Performance Plants
Queen's University, Biosciences Complex,
4th floor
Kingston, ON K7L 3N6
Tel: (613) 545-0390
Fax: (613) 545-3618
http://darwin.biology.queensu.ca/~pplants/
Research and Development
Agriculture

• Lab Manager

David Cameron
Research Manager, Fermentation
Tembec Inc. Chemical Products Group
1 Mill Road, PO Box 3000
Témiscaming, Quebec J0Z 3R0
Tel: (819) 627-4124
Fax: (819) 627-1042
Research and Development
Forestry

• Lab Support

Rebecca Kennedy
Coordinator of Facilities, Purchasing and
Safety
StressGen Biotechnologies Corp.
4243 Glanford Avenue, Suite 350
Victoria, BC V8Z 4B9
Tel: (250) 744-2811
Fax: (250) 744-2877
http://www.stressgen.com/stressgen
Research and Development
Health

• Librarian

Eveline Landa
Head of Information Centre
Biotechnology Research Institute
6100 Royalmount Avenue
Montreal, QC H4P 2R2
Tel: (514) 496-4254
Fax: (514) 496-7885
http://www.nrc.ca/cisti
http://www.bri.nrc.ca/
Adminstration and Regulation

• Patent Agent

Andrew Bauer-Moore
Patent Agent Trainee and Technical
Consultant
Kirby Eades Gale Baker
112 Kent Street, Suite 770
Ottawa, ON K1P 6N9
Tel: (613) 237-6900
Fax: (613) 237-0045
Adminstration and Regulation
Health

• Process Development
Scientist

Yili Bai
Senior Scientist
Phytogen Life Sciences
1527 Cliveden Avenue
Delta, BC V3M 6P7
Tel: (604) 525-5052
Fax: (604) 525-5059
Research and Development
Health

• Product Marketing Manager

Aaron Mitchell
Biotechnology Manager
Monsanto Canada Inc.
206 111 Research Drive, Atrium Building
Saskatoon, SK S7J 3R2
Tel: (306) 975-1327
Fax: (306) 975-1147
http://www.monosanto.com
Sales and Marketing
Agriculture

• Strategic Alliances Manager 102

Duncan Jones
Consultant
Hexagon Innovating
65 Chudleigh Avenue
Toronto, ON M4R 1T4
Tel: (416) 932-9234
 drbjones@home.com
Sales and Marketing
Health

• Toxicologist 130

Catherine Italiano
Toxicologist/Biotechnology Evaluator
Canadian Food Inspection Agency
2001, rue Université
Montreal, QC H3A 3N2
Tel: (514) 283-8888
Fax: (514) 283-3143
http://www.agr.ca
http://www.cfia-aciaagr.ca
Adminstration and Regulation
Agriculture

• University Professor 60

Professor Michael V. Sefton
Department of Chemical Engineering and
Applied Chemistry/Institute of Biomedical
Engineering
University of Toronto
200 College Street
Toronto, ON M5S 1A1
Tel: (416) 978-3088
Fax: (416) 978-8605
http://www.ibme.utoronto.ca
Research and Development
Health

• Veterinarian 62

Daniel Bousquet
Director of Research and Development
L'Alliance Boviteq Inc.
1425, Grand-Rang St-François
St-Hyacinthe, QC J2S 7A9
Tel: (450) 774-7949
Fax: (450) 774-1740
bovi@boviteq.com
Research and Development
Agriculture

CARRIÈRE

Les éditions Ma Carrière

Biotech Career Guide

Editor-in-Chief
Julie Barlow

Assistant to the Editor
Valérie Lapointe
Austin Macdonald

Writers
• Profiles:
Tracey Arial
Sylvain Comeau
Christine Daviault
Janice Paskey
Ingrid Phaneuf
Wallie Seto
Liz Warwick

• Biotech in Focus:
Tracey Arial
Laurie Barlow Cash
Liz Warwick

Correctors
Jennie Anstey
Maria Stuart

Cover design
Lunny Communications
Group

Publication date
March1999

For Les éditions Ma Carrière

Publishers
François Cartier
Marcel Sanscartier

Director of Publications
Patricia Richard

Director of Administrative Services
Nancy Tremblay

Production Coordinator
Valérie Lapointe

Address
5425 de Bordeaux Street,
suite 241
Montreal, QC Canada
H2H 2P9
Tel.: (514) 890-1480
Fax: (514) 890-1456
info@macarriere.net
macarriere.qc.ca

Biotechnology Human
Resource Council (BHRC)
420-130 Albert Street
Ottawa, ON Canada
K1P 5G4
Tel: (613) 235-1402
Fax: (613) 233-7541
www.biotech.ca/bhrc

The Biotech Career Guide
is a publication of the
Biotechnology Human
Resource Council. The
guide was written and
edited by Les éditions Ma
Carrière, in cooperation
with the **National Task
Force for Biotechnology
Career Development**.
Thanks to Task Force
Chair Dennis Fitzpatrick,
and members Balraj Bains,
Jean-Rock Maltais, Réal
Lallier, Phyllis Reardon,
Liette Deschamps, Joyce
Groote and Tanya Soboloff.
Thanks also to Cate
Walker-Hammond, Career
Information Coordinator
for the Career Planning and
Employment Centre at
McMaster University, for
her help gathering career
resources information.

Special thanks to Paul
Watson, Project
Coordinator at BHRC, for
his help, support and
humour!

Legal Deposit
March 1999
National Library of Quebec
ISBN 0-9684482-0-8
National Library of Canada
ISSN 1481-4641

The information in this
publication was up to date
as of December 1998.
The positions of those
interviewed may have
changed since this time.

Copyright© 1999

At **Ma**Carrière

we believe ...

At Les éditions Ma Carrière, we believe that the journey to **success** knows no boundaries. For the past **10 years** we have been helping young Quebecers get a head start on their careers by publishing innovative job guides that provide smart career advice. As **leaders** in our field, we are proud to be expanding on a national level. Based in Montreal, Les éditions Ma Carrière reaches out to more than one million readers annually thanks to our publications many of which have become **best sellers!** Our **experienced** francophone and anglophone editors and contributors are dedicated and team-driven. We are now expanding our reach by publishing books in both languages provincially and Canada-wide. At Les éditions Ma Carrière, our goal is to **keep moving forward.**

These publications were produced by Les éditions Ma Carrière in partnership with the sponsoring agencies.

The Quebec Education System Map
for the Québec Ministry of Education

Vocational Education in School Boards on the Island of Montreal
for the Table régionale de concertation secondaire/collégial de l'île de Montréal

Biotech Career Guide
for the Biotechnology Human Resource Council

Careers in Culture
in partnership with the Cultural Human Resources Council

Canada's Technologist and Technician Career Guide
for the Canadian Technology Human Resources Board

EMC²

Career editions

an imprint of
Les éditions Ma Carrière

The Biotech Career Guide

is
brought
to you
by:

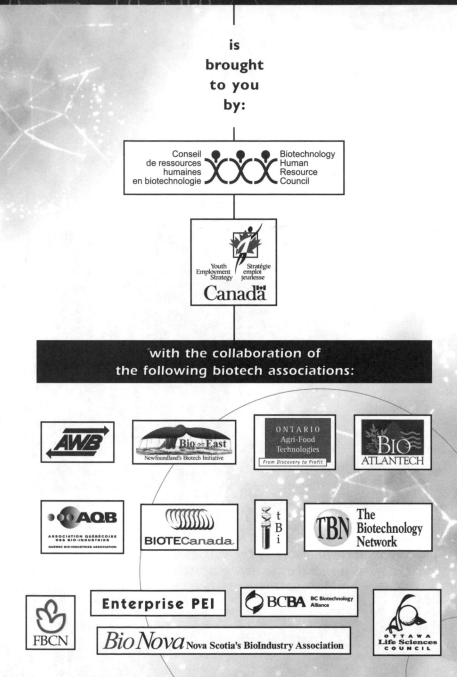

| Conseil de ressources humaines en biotechnologie | Biotechnology Human Resource Council |

Youth Employment Strategy / Stratégie emploi jeunesse
Canada

with the collaboration of the following biotech associations:

AWB

Bio East
Newfoundland's Biotech Initiative

ONTARIO
Agri-Food
Technologies
From Discovery to Profit

BIO
ATLANTECH

AQB
ASSOCIATION QUÉBÉCOISE
DES BIO-INDUSTRIES
QUEBEC BIO-INDUSTRIES ASSOCIATION

BIOTECanada

tBi

TBN The Biotechnology Network

FBCN

Enterprise PEI

BCBA BC Biotechnology Alliance

Bio Nova Nova Scotia's BioIndustry Association

OTTAWA
Life Sciences
COUNCIL

Index
Profiles are listed in alphabetical order according to job title.

161

See page 151 for the Repertoire of Interviewees